# BLACK ROSES

*Steven Downs*

Published by the Press Syndicate of the University of Cambridge
The Pitt Building, Trumpington Street, Cambridge CB2 1RP
40 West 20th Street, New York, NY 10011–4211, USA
10 Stamford Road, Oakleigh, Victoria 3166, Australia

© Cambridge University Press 1992

First published 1992

Printed in Great Britain by Greenshires Print Ltd, Kettering,
Northamptonshire

A catalogue record for this book is available from the British Library

ISBN 0 521 42508 5 paperback

**Performance**
For permission to give a public performance of *Black Roses* please
write to Permissions Department, Cambridge University Press,
The Edinburgh Building, Shaftesbury Road, Cambridge CB2 2RU.

Cover photograph: Press Association/Topham.

GE

# ABOUT THE PLAY

In March 1984 the miners' strike began. It was destined to become one of the longest national strikes in history. Lasting a full year, it had a profound effect on the nation generally, and on many individual mining communities.

It was not a strike over pay, but over pit closures and enforced job losses. These pit closures threatened whole communities and families, and opposition was strong and united. It was different from previous strikes in that family members pulled together. They saw it as a battle for survival and it aroused strong loyalties. It soon became evident that the men alone could not cope with the logistics of organising an effective resistance, and it was at this point that 'Women against Pit Closures' was formed to support the struggle against the government's policy. The year-long strike completely overturned traditional roles and expectations within the communities and, although it ended in failure, many people's lives had been irrevocably changed.

In 1987 the upper sixth theatre studies group of Shelley High School began research for their group project. After interviewing a group of miners' wives from Woolley, their research was turned into a full-length play. *Black Roses* looks at the problems faced by the women from the first day of the strike until its collapse a year later – problems that were generated not just by the government, Coal Board or police but also by the unions, the menfolk and their families.

The lasting impression held by the students was of a group of women whose lives had been indelibly scarred by the hardship of the strike, but who had also undergone a more positive kind of change, through the realisation of their own potential.

In 1988 Woolley colliery closed as an uneconomic pit. Some miners found jobs in nearby pits, some took voluntary redundancy and a few remained as a skeleton staff to wind up the pit.

# CHARACTERS

RAY — miner, Christine's husband
BRIAN — miner, Sandra's husband
DAVE — miner, Doreen's husband
FRANK — miner
GOVERNMENT OFFICIAL

SANDRA
CHRISTINE
DOREEN
BETTY SHARP } Miners' Wives
MARGARET } Support Group
MAUREEN
JOAN

JACK WOODHEAD — NUM local branch secretary
REPORTERS 1–3
TRACEY LOCKWOOD — 14, Doreen's daughter
MINERS 1 & 2
POLICE INSPECTOR
POLICEMEN 1 & 2
MALCOLM — painter and decorator
ARTHUR — bus driver
WELSH WIFE
BANK MANAGER
WELFARE LADY
SOCIAL SECURITY WORKER
SOCIAL WORKER
RICHARD WOOD — son of Brian and Sandra
KIRSTY WOOD — daughter of Brian and Sandra
JACKIE CLAYTON — comedian
MARVO THE MAGICIAN
FATHER CHRISTMAS

# PRODUCTION NOTE

*Black Roses* was first performed at Shelley High School on Tuesday 1 March 1988. The production was an 'ensemble' production, with each member of the cast playing four or five characters in turn. The original cast was: Vicky Ellam, Kati Haigh, Fiona Holt, Gill Inglis, Helen Loughlin, Mandy Lumsden, Liz Paterson and Imogen Priest.

The musicians were: Emma Kaye, Nicola Paterson, Daniel Priest, Daniel McKinna, Jeremy Raby and Darren Wood. The music was arranged by Darren Wood. The play was produced by Steven Downs and Jacqui Gill.


# STAGE DIRECTIONS

There are two kinds of directions in this playscript. Those in **bold type** provide information that is essential to an understanding of what is happening in the play at the time. For a play-reading, these should be read by a separate reader.

Those in *italic type* are less essential stage directions and offer suggestions to assist with a production of the play onstage. In a reading they are best not read out as they will hamper the flow of the play, although those who are reading may find that some of these instructions offer help with the interpretation of their lines.

*Black Roses* has a cast of over thirty characters. As can be seen from the original cast list, it is possible to perform the piece using only eight actors. If this ensemble style is adopted, it does present certain challenges, particularly with crowd scenes. It is, however, possible with creative directing to devise exciting and interesting ways of representing crowds and the like. The ensemble style gives the script a much tighter feel and the pace is consequently improved. Because the play is open to so many different staging options, I have avoided, wherever possible, very detailed stage directions.

**SCENE 1**

Band plays quietly. Lights come up to low on four MINERS who mime shovelling and picking coal. A bowler-hatted OFFICIAL enters and briefly consults a clipboard. He marks a cross on the clipboard, then points at the first miner who slows to a halt. The official repeats the process until the other three miners are all still. The official surveys the scene with some satisfaction and then exits. The miners remain isolated in the dim light. Music builds. The miners reach to link hands but cannot make the connection. Three WOMEN enter and place themselves between the men. The gaps are thus filled and they are all able to link hands and form a chain. Music crescendo. Lights up and then dim to black-out.

**SCENE 2**

**BRIAN and RAY are sitting with cups of tea, which they keep lifting to their lips, but never drinking.**

SANDRA & CHRISTINE   Strike!

BRIAN & RAY   Aye. Strike.

SANDRA   I knew it'd come to this . . . another bloody strike. By hell, am I sick of strikes.

BRIAN   Nay, come on, love. We've balloted against last two what were proposed.

CHRISTINE   Did they not ballot against it again?

RAY   We haven't had a chance yet, love. That's probably to come once Union's organised.

SANDRA   Oh, that's alright. We'll all be dead by then.

BRIAN   No, it's serious this time, love. Board have drawn up a list of uneconomic pits. They reckon they're gonna close dozens.

CHRISTINE   Does this mean there's no money at all coming in?

*Scene 2*  7

RAY  I'm afraid so. There might be a bit of strike money and they're talking about paying for picketing, but it's peanuts. Don't worry, love, if all goes well, it should be over in a fortnight.

SANDRA  And how the hell am I gonna manage for a fortnight wi' no money coming in? I'm not a magician, Brian. I can't pull pork chops out of a bloody top hat.

BRIAN  We'll just have to pull back a bit, that's all. We've a bit in the bank we can draw on.

CHRISTINE  That's our holiday money, Ray.

RAY  I know, love, but we'll not need it all. We'll soon make up for it. Anyway, we've no choice. I can't go into work on me own.

SANDRA  So, on top of everything else, I'm going to have you getting under me feet all day, am I?

BRIAN  No. I'll be out picketing most days.

CHRISTINE  Well, I suppose we'll get some of these jobs done at home.

RAY  Aye, I'll be around a bit more.

SANDRA  I don't know. We're all just too eager to down tools at slightest excuse wi'out a minute's thought about how we'll manage.

BRIAN  Don't be daft, course we've thought about it. But we've thought further than where the housekeeping brass is coming from for the next fortnight. We've got to nip this closure business in the bud or else there's no telling how it'll spread – it could be us next.

CHRISTINE  You don't think so, do you, love?

RAY  There's no telling. Anyhow, you needn't worry yourself about it. Union men'll sort it out.

SANDRA  And what happens if it don't end in a fortnight? Supposing it goes on longer?

8   *Black Roses*

BRIAN  It'll not. Once Board realises strength of the feeling they'll be forced to capitulate.

CHRISTINE  I hate strikes, Ray. It frightens me when you can't see an end to it.

RAY  I know, love, but it shouldn't be too bad. Everybody's coming out all over the country, apparently. Board'll not stand up to that sort of pressure for long.

SANDRA  By bloody hell . . . I wish I had your faith in the power of the unions.

BRIAN  It's different this time. Union's really united on this one. It's not just like a pay or conditions strike, isn't this. This is fighting for us jobs, for us fundamental right to work.

CHRISTINE  I don't really understand it all, I must admit, but I'm sure you're right.

RAY  You know, you could help in this if you wanted. Some women down at the club said they were thinking of starting a support group and they were looking for members.

SANDRA  Them Union men can't organise their own backsides. They're shed pigeons, that lot. You'll get nowhere with them. I tell yer, I could do better than that lot of slack Alices.

BRIAN  Hey up then, you want to put your money where your mouth is, you do. Betty Sharp's thinking of starting a women's strike group and she's looking for volunteers. Tha wants to get round.

SANDRA  I don't think I'd like that much. It's not my scene that.

RAY  You get down there, get involved. It'll be better than hanging round the house worrying all day.

SANDRA  I think I just might. It's a good idea, is that. She's a bit of a tartar, is Betty, but she'll get things moving.

BRIAN  You can say that again.

| | |
|---|---|
| SANDRA | Aye, it's a good idea, is that. |
| BRIAN & RAY | Right. (*Both lift their teacups to their lips, and drink.*) Urgh! Have you sugared this tea? |
| SANDRA | I might have forgotten, love. D'you mind fetching it yourself, this time? |
| CHRISTINE | Hey, if we're fighting this job together, we're on equal terms. Go fetch your own bloody sugar. |

**(SANDRA and CHRISTINE link hands.)**

## SCENE 3

**There is chaos: noise and movement. Enter BETTY SHARP with JACK WOODHEAD, the Union man.**

| | |
|---|---|
| BETTY SHARP | Right, come on then, shut up. Let's have a bit of hush. Shut it! |
| | **(The meeting quietens.)** |
| | Right then, let's get started. We all know why we're here, don't we? |
| SANDRA | Aye, it's a good excuse to get out for a drink wi'out our Brian tagging on. (*General laughter*) |
| BETTY SHARP | Alright, it might be that for some people. For others of us it's a bit more serious. |
| CHRISTINE | Why? Is there bingo? (*Laughter*) |
| BETTY SHARP | No, I'm afraid there's no bingo. (*All groan.*) We've got Jack here from NUM local branch . . . |
| DOREEN | Hey up, a male stripper, girls. (*Cheers from the other women.*) Get'em off, darling. |
| BETTY SHARP | As I was saying, Jack's here to discuss with us the role of our women's support group, as seen overall in the total strike effort, as it were. I think as women we've got to organise ourselves into a group and offer our services to |

10    *Black Roses*

Jack . . . (*Loud cheers of 'Lucky Jack!', 'Can you manage us all Jack!', 'Jack the lad!', etc.*) Alright, you know what I mean. Take no notice of 'em Jack they're allus like this. Anyway, all us that's here are here because we want to help, because we want to support our husbands and sons in the strike in any way we can . . . so . . . well I'll hand over to you, Jack. (*The women cheer and clap.*)

JACK    (*Embarrassed*) Right then, ladies. Right. I must say I'm very pleased to have been invited here tonight by . . . er . . .

BETTY SHARP    Betty!

JACK    Aye, Betty. And it's grand to see so many lasses here what's . . . er . . . what's interested enough in what's going on to want to become involved, and that. We, as a union, very much appreciate the support of our womenfolk and I'm sure your contributions are going to be most valuable.

SANDRA    Come on, Jack lad. Get on with it.

JACK    Aye, right. Well thank you. Right, well . . . er . . . it has been put to the Union committee local branch, like, that there are a lot of ladies willing to help wi' the strike effort and committee has discussed it at some length and we've given the matter some considerable thought, like, and it seems to us that your services would be most valuable in manning the soup kitchens for the pickets. You know, cooking and serving lunches and that and . . . er . . . helping clear up after, like.

(**Silence. Women look round.**)

SANDRA    Is that it, then?

JACK    Aye.

DOREEN    And how many hours of considerable thought and deep discussion did it take you to come to that conclusion?

CHRISTINE    Well done, Jack and the Union committee. What a brilliant strategy.

*Scene 3* **11**

| | |
|---|---|
| JACK | Nay, it were obvious really. You'll serve a very useful purpose there, ladies. Lads were very grateful for your offer. They wondered if you'd be able to organise a rota of some sort so some of you can be cooking whilst others run a sort of creche thing for the kiddies. |
| MARGARET | Is that the bloody best you could come up with? |
| JACK | Why? What's up? What did you expect? |
| MARGARET | What we expected, Jack, was that somebody might take us seriously, that we'd be found summat useful to do, summat that would make a real difference to the strike effort. |
| JACK | Well, this is it. |
| CHRISTINE | Bollocks, Jack. Cooking and washing-up, again. I've enough cooking and washing-up to do at home. We want to get involved, Jack, on equal terms wi' the men . . . not just the usual skivvying about. |
| JACK | Hey, come on, girls. I mean, fair's fair. I mean, let's keep a sense of perspective. What sort of thing did you have in mind? |
| BETTY SHARP | That's what we asked you and the committee to decide, Jack. |
| JACK | Well, we have. We've decided where your contribution would be most valuable in our opinion. |
| BETTY SHARP | Well, we think your idea's crap, Jack. We're offering our wholehearted support in the struggle, and you offer us bloody washing-up. |
| JACK | Come on, Betty, be fair. What can you do? |
| CHRISTINE | What can we do? We can do owt you buggers on the committee can do. And more besides. |
| JACK | Don't be daft. You can't go picketing, for a start. |
| DOREEN | Why not? |
| JACK | 'Cos it's hard, unpleasant, cold, and it can be dangerous. |

12   *Black Roses*

DOREEN   So?

JACK   So it's a man's job.

BETTY SHARP   Rubbish.

JACK   It's not rubbish. You've no idea. Things are getting bloody nasty out there.

BETTY SHARP   Things are gonna get bloody nasty in here, Jack, if you carry on.

SANDRA   Look, Jack, can't yer see? Here we are offering help. We're willing to do anything, within reason, and all you're saying is do the washing-up, girls.

JACK   And cooking.

SANDRA   Oh piss off.

BETTY SHARP   Look, Jack. What would you give us to do if we were a bunch of blokes offering to help . . . eh? Just forget we're women.

JACK   How can I do that? Women are women, blokes is blokes.

CHRISTINE   Oh, God help us!

JACK   Look, girls, be reasonable. Every little bit helps and when these lads come in from picketing, they'll be starving. It might seem a small insignificant job to you, but take it from me, it'll be much appreciated by the pickets.

MAUREEN   Jack lad, you haven't been blessed wi' cosmic vision have you?

JACK   What are you talking about now?

MAUREEN   Well, here you are being offered the services of innumerable willing helpers and, because they're women, you automatically think cooking and washing-up's the limit of their contributions.

JACK   Well, what do you suggest then? Pickets have to be fed.

*Scene 3*  **13**

SANDRA We don't disagree with that. We're not objecting to doing it. We're mad because that's *all* you think we can do.

JACK What else is there? You tell me.

CHRISTINE There's fund-raising, for a start.

JACK Funds? What for? Union's got all the money it needs.

CHRISTINE Aye, it has now. But what if the strike goes on a month or two, or even six, then what? You'll be feeling the pinch then, and so will we.

JACK It'll not go so long. Board'll not face up to the full weight of the Union for long.

DOREEN Full weight less Nottingham, Jack.

SANDRA Aye, you never know. It's spring now. There's plenty of coal stocks. If you ask me the Board could sit this out for a while. And if Union has any sense it'll start thinking of this as a long-term struggle.

BETTY SHARP We can mobilise the women in this area, Jack, into a right good support group. And we're not in any mood to be palmed off with just bloody skivvying for the pickets.

MARGARET Hey, there's a soup kitchen for the pickets. Is the Union setting up one for the pickets' families?

JACK No, course not. Union can only finance its own members, them as is actively engaged in lawful picketing.

MARGARET Right then, that's summat we can do. We'll open a soup kitchen for women and kids of the miners, 'cos if this strike job drags on there's going to be a need for it. (*Women nod and murmur agreement.*)

JACK And how are you going to run that? Union'll not be able or willing to finance it.

BETTY SHARP Don't worry, Jack. We won't need Union money. That's what we've been trying to tell you. We're more than capable of coping for ourselves.

14    *Black Roses*

CHRISTINE    We can raise money with jumble sales.

SANDRA    Collections and that . . . maybe concerts.

DOREEN    Local shops and that might help.

JACK    Hey, just hold on. This isn't a game, this strike job, tha knows. You can't just go flitting about countryside playing at Florence Nightingale. Union has got this job organised. Any support it needs from you I've already outlined. Men on picketing, them's number one priority, never mind opening bloody soup kitchens and coffee shops. Jumble sales and collecting . . . it's a load of nonsense. I tell you, leave the bloody thinking and organising to us lads. We're the ones who's trained in this sort of thing. Pull together, each to his or her own job, not all running round like headless chickens getting in each other's way.

BETTY SHARP    Jack, we've said we'll support you. We'll feed your pickets, but we're not stopping at that. You've underestimated women badly. It's all the community that's under threat here and so it's all the community that's gonna fight. We're ready and willing to get involved and we will do, with or without Union's backing. And I'll tell you summat, Jack, you'll be looking at us through different eyes by the time this job's over.

**SCENE 4**

Soup kitchen. General activity – carrying of pans to and fro.

BETTY SHARP    So that's finance committee sorted out, planning and cooking teams. Mary, how did you get on wi' the allotment folk?

SANDRA    They were great. There's not a lot now wi' it being season's end, but there's about a dozen what have agreed to form a group. We've offered 'em help for seeds and that. In return we'll get all the produce when the time comes.

*Scene 4*  **15**

CHRISTINE   I hope it'll all be over by then.

SANDRA   Aye, well you never know. It'll do no harm to plan ahead.

BETTY SHARP   You're right. Now, Doreen, what about financing?

DOREEN   Well, we've sent off the application form for street-collecting and we're planning house-to-house collecting, so that's taken care of, we've plenty of volunteers for that. Co-op manager's given us permission to set up a collecting point in the shop foyer. We'll collect food and money there. We want more folk for that, though. We reckon two, on a three-hour shift.

BETTY SHARP   That's not asking too much.

DOREEN   Money and food must be parcelled up and the total value must be less than £4. If it's over, then DHSS classify it as income and knock it off benefit.

SANDRA   Bloody hell, I'd be owing them if they knocked it off mine.

BETTY SHARP   Cooking seems taken care of. Union's creamed off a lot for the pickets' kitchen, but we've enough to manage if we organise usselves.

SANDRA   Yeah, kitchen's going well now.

CHRISTINE   Except silly bugger Joan put salt in the custard instead of sugar.

JOAN   (*Just passing through with pans*) I couldn't help it, hadn't got me specs on. Salt looks like sugar when you haven't got your specs on.

SANDRA   You'll have to taste it in future, Joan.

JOAN   Alright, clever bugger, it's alright being wise after the event.

BETTY SHARP   Aye. Well everything's not gonna run smoothly at first. We're all new to this job so we'll have to learn by us mistakes. We don't want no falling out though, we've to

16    *Black Roses*

pull together, remember. 'United we stand, divided we fall'. While we're united we'll do alright.

CHRISTINE    Unless Joan poisons us all . . . (*Joan gestures and exits.*)

SANDRA    You know, it's great, this . . . I mean, I know it's hard wi' the strike and that, but don't you get a great feeling when you come down here and you see everyone pulling together like this . . . you know, getting involved . . . it's brilliant.

BETTY SHARP    Aye, it's a chance for us, is this, a chance to prove to the men we've got a bit about us . . . we're not just washers-up and child-bearers. We've got to make a go of it.

DOREEN    It's important to you is this, isn't it, Betty?

BETTY SHARP    It is, yeah. I've always been aware, ever since I was young, that men never took me seriously – you know what I mean – any opinions or ideas I've had when I've spoken out, they've allus been put down. Right from school it's been the same . . . my dad, teachers, blokes I've been out with and even our Bob, especially our Bob. You know, you try to talk to 'em about summat important – summat besides the kids or the house – and they clam up. 'Gi' us a kiss, love.' 'Don't you worry about that.' Or they just yawn and say 'Are you coming up to bed?' I've allus felt I've got so much to give, like an energy in here (*Taps heart*) and ideas and that, I'm just bursting with 'em. And now I've got a chance to use it all, to break out . . .

(**There is an explosion off-stage.**)

ALL    Bloody hell, what's that? Good God (*etc.*)

(**Enter JOAN shocked.**)

JOAN    Oh my God . . . Gi' me some air.

SANDRA    What is it, Joan?

DOREEN    Are you alright?

CHRISTINE    What happened?

*Scene 4*  **17**

JOAN  It's me rice pudding. I put it in a glass casserole in the oven and all the lot's blown up. Bloody oven's dripping wi' rice pudding.

SANDRA  Oh no! Was it a pyrex you put it in?

JOAN  No, it were a durex. D'yer think I'm bloody daft?

CHRISTINE  I'm saying nowt.

JOAN  Course it were a pyrex. I looked before I put it in.

SANDRA  Did you have your specs on?

JOAN  Get stuffed.

BETTY SHARP  Come on, it don't matter. This sort of thing's gonna happen. We've not got to let it upset us. Come on, let's get stuck in.

SANDRA  Come on, Joan – remember. (*Sings*) 'I am strong, I am invincible, I am Woman'.

JOAN  What's that?

SANDRA  Helen Reddy – 'I am Woman'. Do you know it?

CHRISTINE  I've got it on an LP. It's brilliant.

DOREEN  How does it go?

SANDRA  'I am strong.'

CHRISTINE  'Strong.'

SANDRA  'I am invincible.'

CHRISTINE  'Invincible.'

SANDRA &  'I am Woman.'
CHRISTINE

SANDRA &  (*Sing*) I am Woman, hear me roar
CHRISTINE  In numbers too big to ignore
And I know too much to go back to pretend
'Cause I've heard it all before
And I've been down there on the floor
No one's ever gonna keep me down again.

18     *Black Roses*

(SANDRA and CHRISTINE sing the chorus – encouraging the others who join in hesitantly.)

Oh yes, I am wise but it's wisdom born of pain
Yes I've paid the price
But look how much I've gained
If I have to, I can do anything
I am strong.

ALL     (*Providing their own echo*) STRONG
I am invincible
INVINCIBLE
I am Woman.

SANDRA &     You can bend but never break me (*band join in*)
CHRISTINE     'Cause it only serves to make me
More determined to reach my final goal
And I come back even stronger
Not a novice any longer
'Cause you've deepened the conviction in my soul.

ALL     (*Sing chorus with confidence*)
Oh yes, I am wise but it's wisdom born of pain
Yes I've paid the price
But look how much I've gained
If I have to, I can do anything
I am strong
STRONG
I am invincible
INVINCIBLE
I am Woman.

## SCENE 5

REPORTER 1     Can you tell me what the role of the women's support group will be?

BETTY SHARP     To support the men in their fight against pit closures and to provide help for their families.

REPORTER 2     What form will this support and help take?

*Scene 5*  **19**

CHRISTINE   We're setting up a soup kitchen for the women and kids. Hopefully, if donations keep coming in, we'll be handing out food parcels and even clothing, if necessary.

REPORTER 3   Will you be involving yourselves in any more direct ways?

SANDRA   What can be more direct than that? We'll be working direct with families and helping them through what'll be a very difficult time.

REPORTER 1   How far are you prepared to go in your struggle?

BETTY SHARP   As far as we need to go to provide and survive. We'll be organising street-collections, charity events, fund-raising, so on and so forth. We also hope to provide advice for people who are having difficulties with mortgages and other payments.

REPORTER 2   Anything else?

CHRISTINE   Organising social events to bring people together. It could be a long hard struggle, could this, and we need unity. Folk need to know they're not alone in their hardship. We've to draw the community together.

REPORTER 3   Do you see your role changing at all?

SANDRA   Definitely. We've never really had a challenge like this before. A real cause to fight for. It's opening our eyes, is this. We've always been content with what we've got, and suddenly it's all being taken from us. It's woken things in me I never knew existed!

REPORTER 1   What about even more front-line involvement, like on the picket lines? Will you involve yourselves in that?

BETTY SHARP   We will be involved in all aspects of the strike, although us main contribution will be what I've said already – supporting families. We may well help out, if necessary, on the picket lines.

REPORTER 2   And what about the violence on the picket lines? Doesn't that frighten you?

20    *Black Roses*

BETTY SHARP    It doesn't frighten us, flower. No.

REPORTER 3    So if there was violence, would you involve yourself?

BETTY SHARP    Put it this way, love, we've some pretty formidable ladies living round here, and if anybody tried to give 'em a hard time, they'd get more than they bargained for.

REPORTERS    Thank you, ladies, you've been very helpful. Good luck, girls. (*Reporters huddle to side of stage.*)

BETTY SHARP    Well, how do you think we did?

CHRISTINE    Alright, I think. I were surprised. Words seemed to come out so easy.

SANDRA    That's because we believe in what we're doing. We've thought it through.

CHRISTINE    When you put it in words . . . all of it, though . . . it seems really . . . I don't know . . . noble . . . doesn't it?

BETTY SHARP    Yeah . . . When people read that, it ought to get us a lot of support.

REPORTER 1    What do you think?

REPORTER 2    It's all a bit . . . noble.

**(Pause. Others nod in agreement.)**

REPORTER 3    How about 'Pithead Amazons pledge violence'?

**(REPORTERS exit nodding in agreement.)**


**SCENE 6**

**Enter TRACEY. She flings down her schoolbag and sits down heavily.**

DOREEN    (*Sarcastically*) Nice day, dear?

TRACEY    No.

DOREEN    What's up?

TRACEY    Everything.

*Scene 6* **21**

| | |
|---|---|
| DOREEN | What do you mean, love? |
| TRACEY | It doesn't matter. (*Gets up.*) |
| DOREEN | Tracey, love. it does matter. Come on, talk to me, love. |
| TRACEY | It don't matter! |
| DOREEN | Love, it's no good bottling it up. If you've something to say, out with it . . . Is it trouble at school? . . . Tracey? |
| TRACEY | Yeah . . . sort of . . . |
| DOREEN | What sort of? Kids or teachers? |
| TRACEY | It's nowt, Mam. |
| DOREEN | TRACEY! |
| TRACEY | I just got in a bit of bother today . . . for cheeking a teacher. |
| DOREEN | Tracey! |
| TRACEY | Well, it wasn't my fault. She asked for it . . . rotten bitch. |
| DOREEN | Hey, that's enough of that . . . Who are you talking about, anyway? |
| TRACEY | That Mrs Ramsden – Head of our Year. |
| DOREEN | And what's that poor woman done to deserve the rough end of your tongue? |
| TRACEY | Poor woman nothing, she's a cow! |
| DOREEN | Alright, calm down and tell me what's up! |
| TRACEY | It were about them free dinners. |
| DOREEN | What about 'em? |
| TRACEY | Well, we have to collect these tokens on a Monday morning, one for each day of the week and when I went for mine, she starts going on about miners' strike and that, and how her taxes shouldn't be used to finance a communist uprising. |
| DOREEN | She what? |

22    *Black Roses*

TRACEY    She did, Mam. She were shouting and carrying on about miners sponging and how it were a disgrace and in the end she just threw my tokens on the floor and told me to pick 'em up.

DOREEN    The rotten bitch. What did you do?

TRACEY    I were really upset, Mam, and mad. I started crying and shouting back at her. I told her she could stuff her free meals and her taxes. I told her it wasn't me on strike. I hadn't chosen it. If she felt like that she could go down and shout at Union.

DOREEN    Good for you, girl. I've a good mind to go up to that school and complain about her to the Headmaster. She's no right to go on like that.

TRACEY    Aw, Mam, don't do that please. Don't cause no more trouble. She'll only make things more difficult for me another time. I'm in enough bother.

DOREEN    Alright, love, but if there's out else like that you come straight and tell me. I'm not having it.

TRACEY    Alright, Mam.

DOREEN    The cheeky cow . . . it makes me sick. Come on, love . . . cheer up, now.

TRACEY    Mam?

DOREEN    What love?

TRACEY    Is there any chance I can go on a theatre trip wi' drama club? Mr Bentley's taking us to Leeds Playhouse to see this comedy. He says it's really funny and we should try and get if we can manage 'cos we can write it up for us files and everyone else's going so . . .

DOREEN    Tracey, love . . . Tracey . . . how much is it?

TRACEY    £5.50, including coach.

DOREEN    Oh Tracey, love . . . we can't manage that . . . honestly.

TRACEY    But Mam, everybody's going.

*Scene 6* **23**

DOREEN   I know, love, but everybody's not on chuffing strike, are they?

TRACEY   No!

DOREEN   Tracey . . . look, love, you know how things are. We're living on a damned pittance and until this job's sorted out, we're all going to have to cut back, make sacrifices and I'm afraid that going to the theatre is a luxury we can't afford no more.

TRACEY   I'm sick of this. It's not fair.

DOREEN   Tracey!

TRACEY   Well it's not. It's always the same . . . I can't do this . . . I can't do that. All my mates are going here and there and getting new clothes and that, and me, I'm stuck here. I can't go nowhere because we can't afford bus fare. I can't have any new clothes, can't go on the school trips . . . have to join free-dinner queues, get slanged off all the time and all because of a bloody stupid strike about nothing, what's not going to work anyhow. I'm sick of it. I wish they'd just go back . . .

DOREEN   Don't you dare talk like that! Who the hell do you think you are? It's not a bloody stupid strike. It's a very important strike. It's a strike for your future, and because of that it's got to succeed. That's why everybody's pulling together. Men and women alike, because they know that's the only way they'll win. It's going to mean hardships and sacrifices from everybody. We've had it easy up to now. We've always had enough money for luxuries and that, which is going to make it harder now the crunch has come.

TRACEY   (*A little truculently*) I'm sorry.

DOREEN   Oh Tracey, I do know how difficult it is for you, love. I can't explain how important this is – not properly, I don't think – but it is, love, believe me. It tears me apart inside when I have to say no to you all the time. I know what you're going through but I can't give in, neither

24    *Black Roses*

can your dad. We've got to support him and each other, or else there'll be no future for us, love. D'you see?

TRACEY    Yes, I suppose so.

DOREEN    I hope you'll understand, love . . . perhaps when you're a bit older. The trouble is, just now clothes and trips and friends are much more important than political struggles, aren't they?

TRACEY    I don't know.

DOREEN    Course they are. It wouldn't be right if they weren't. But one day you'll realise what I've been trying to say. You'll know it were right. But till then, love, you'll just have to trust me and do your best. (*She holds hands with Tracey*.) We're all united in this. It'll bring us closer together and we'll win in the end, despite all yer Mrs Ramsdens.


**SCENE 7**

MAUREEN is shaking a collecting tin. A few passers-by avoid her.

MARGARET    Support the miners' families. Thank you. Please give generously. Support the miners' families. Support the miners in their struggle. Help stop pit closures. Support the miners' families.

(Enter MAUREEN.)

MAUREEN    (*Mimicking*) Oh, my dear, I am an eccentric millionaire from Featherstone. Do take this cheque for £100,000, with my best wishes.

MARGARET    Oh no, not another bloody eccentric millionaire. That's the eighth this morning. Thank you, sir, we'll invest your donation in Japanese unit trusts and one hundred families will live like lords off the interest.

MAUREEN    Well done, my girl, keep up the good work. (*She reverts to self*.) How much, then?

*Scene 7*  **25**

MARGARET Not too bad. I don't know exactly – £25–£30, maybe. I'll tell you what, though, if I got a quid for every dirty look and a fiver for nasty comments, we'd be able to buy the NCB out, and keep it running usselves.

MAUREEN Not so good, eh?

MARGARET No, I hate it. I mean some folk are alright, you know – especially old'uns. They don't give much, but they allus have a word. But there are some miserable buggers in this town. A lot just walk straight past you as if you didn't exist. I've even seen some cross over the street to avoid us.

MAUREEN Aye, I know. It's just as bad on the door to door. Some are fine and some . . . well you know they're in, but you could bray on the door all day and they wouldn't come. One got me really mad this morning. I saw her face behind the curtain when I walked up the path and I rang and rang on the bell, but she would hell as like come . . . hiding under the bed. In the end I were that mad I just lifted letter-flap up and shouted 'I hope you get your head stuck in the jerry yer miserable cow.' I were blazing.

MARGARET Police come up to me first thing this morning, nasty as hell . . . asked to see me permit. They said I wasn't to approach people or even rattle me tin. Then they sat in the noddy car on there, just watching me all the time.

MAUREEN It's a pity they've nowt better to do. We went into a shop this morning just to ask for a donation and that, and the bloke went mad . . . said he'd call the coppers if we didn't get out.

MARGARET The rotten sod.

MAUREEN Oh, there's a lot like that. They forget it's been miners what's brought 'em all their trade in the past.

MARGARET Aye, and they forget that strike'll end one day and there'll be no miners going in their shops then.

MAUREEN Aye, that's right, the miserable buggers they are!
I wonder where it's all gonna end?

26    *Black Roses*

MARGARET    Where and when.

MAUREEN    Aye.

MARGARET    I'm sick of it all now. I mean, when we're all together in the kitchen and that, and singing, it's great. I love that. You feel like you'll never be beaten. But then again, you get out here and it's cold and pissing down, you're on yer own and nobody wants to know. That's when it's hard, Maureen.

MAUREEN    I know, love. It's hard and it's going to get bloody harder. But we will do it in the end. When yer think about women's organisation and that – how much we're managing to do – it's fantastic.

MARGARET    Yeah. I just sometimes get this feeling like everything's closing in and we'll just be crushed. A bloke come up to me this morning, right well spoken he was, an' he says 'You've got all my support, my dear. The struggle you're involved in is a very important one. It is imperial, or summat, that we succeed, and he slipped me a fiver and patted my hand and went off. An' I thought . . . aye, it's alright giving a fiver and talking like that, but that's all in this 'very important struggle' that bugger's willing to risk. He'll have given a fiver out of about 20,000 he'll earn this year and gone away thinking 'Let them silly sods fight on for my cause.' He'll not be going cold and hungry for his cause, will he? Bloody champagne-socialist. I reckon they're worse'n Tories . . . hypocrites, they are.

MAUREEN    I know what you mean, love, but he's right in a way, I suppose. I mean we're like front-line troops, so it's us that's going to suffer more during the struggle . . . but then again afterwards it'll be us what's getting all the glory.

MARGARET    Yeah . . . it just sickens me off, all the pressure all the time – at home, and here – struggling to make ends meet. Everybody's getting frustrated. When we started all the women were right enthusiastic. We were carried along 'cos it were summat new and exciting and different. Now we seem to be making no progress. I mean, how much longer can we expect people to put money in us tins? How much longer can we take all the harassment? Same wi' the men, Unions is getting nowhere. It's all a big volcano boiling up inside. It frightens me, Maureen. Where's it all gonna end?

**SCENE 8**

Loud noisy crowd comes in quickly. Company split into POLICE and MINERS. They face up to one another.

MINER 1   We can't win Nottingham, we've got to accept that. The police learnt the lessons from '72 and '74 – the lessons we haven't learnt – and they've got Nottingham sewn up. The question that's got to be raised is Orgreave. Orgreave is a focal point for this strike. It's not just a question of stopping twenty lorries of coke. A victory at Orgreave would turn this struggle completely upside down into a victory for us.
*(Cheering from the miners)*

MINER 2   We've got to step up the tempo of the dispute. I want to see every single miner on the picket line. If that means you get arrested, you'll have to accept the consequences. We're in this to the finish.

POLICE
INSPECTOR   We were faced with the alternative – either stop mass picketing or lose the initiative completely. The closure of Orgreave might have been the start of a lot of closures.

(The following scene becomes a series of posed tableaux, created by freezing the riot action every time a character addresses the audience. The intervening bouts of activity are frenzied.)

MINERS   Here we go, here we go, here we go (*etc.*)

POLICE
INSPECTOR   Stand firm . . . close ranks . . . hold them there. (*Pause*) Number One Snatch Squad Target and go.

(Police break forward – and grab a miner.)

28   *Black Roses*

BRIAN   They came from nowhere. One minute I were having a laugh, singing and chanting with me mates, the next I were down under all them pigs. They knocked seven bells outa me, kept calling me a bastard. 'You'll never walk again, you bastard' one said. He were hammering at me legs with his stick. Another just pulled me head back by me hair and punched me in the face.

POLICE   RE-FORM!
INSPECTOR

(Police line up. Miners chant 'Sieg Heil' and start to push against the shields.)

POLICEMAN 1   Hey, bastards, you want to keep this up – I drew 500 quid last week, thanks to you dozy sods. What did you draw?

RAY   He kept goading me. I couldn't stand it, I just went for him. I had to get at him.

POLICE   Target and go.
INSPECTOR

(Police line opens. Miner falls in.)

RAY   I suddenly realised I were in trouble. I've never been so scared. I thought they were gonna kill me. Later, when I got home, I noticed my jeans and T-shirt were covered in black marks. I realised later it were boot polish.

(Police line re-forms. Miners push against police.)

DAVE   We were caught between the coppers, and pickets pushing from the back. We hadn't a chance against shields and riot sticks. And to make matters worse stones being thrown from the back were falling on us.

(Miners continue chanting and pushing. Police advance. Miners retreat. A gap appears. Miners scatter.)

DAVE   When things were at their worst they pulled back and apart and mounted police came galloping through – a full-blooded cavalry charge, batons drawn – there were mass panic. It were bloody terrifying.

*Scene 8* **29**

(Police 'gallop' through. One goes to strike a fleeing miner with his baton.)

DAVE  I just ran – anywhere to get out the way. I heard this galloping behind me and then it seemed like me head exploded.

POLICE INSPECTOR  Re-form . . . advance.

(GOVERNMENT OFFICIAL steps from police ranks as fights break out.)

GOVERN-MENT OFFICIAL  We have to make it clear that violence is totally unacceptable in our society.

(Fighting resumes.)

GOVERN-MENT OFFICIAL  The British police do not have sophisticated riot equipment to handle demonstrations. The traditional approach is to deploy large numbers of officers in ordinary uniform in passive containment of a crowd. Neither the Government nor the police wish to see this approach abandoned in favour of more aggressive methods.

(Fighting resumes.)

GOVERN-MENT OFFICIAL  In the Falklands we had to fight the enemy without. Here the enemy is within and it is much more difficult to fight, but just as dangerous to liberty.

(Miner walks casually past the fighting, which this time continues as he speaks.)

MALCOLM  I was just coming back from me allotment. I had to go up our street. It were swarming wi' police and miners. (*Police grab Malcolm.*) Suddenly I'm grabbed . . . Gerroff, I say . . .

POLICEMAN 1  Let me see your hands.

MALCOLM  Me hands? I says.

POLICEMAN 1  Dirty . . . another bloody stone-thrower.

30   *Black Roses*

MALCOLM   Hey up . . . they're dirty 'cos I've been in me allotment. I'm not even a bloody miner . . . I'm a painter and decorator.

POLICEMAN 2   Bang the bastard up!

(**Police withdraw leaving miners battered.**)

BRIAN   What a mess that day was – a complete cock-up.

RAY   They were out to maim that day, not just arrest.

DAVE   And we fell right into the trap. We were mugs.

BRIAN   Come on Ray let's get you to the infirmary. You want looking at.

FRANK   (*Enters*) Hey up, lads, don't go in there. Pigs is in there just arresting any miners what goes in for treatment.

BRIAN   Bloody hell . . . come on then, let's get back home and patched up.

RAY   Our lass'll kill me when she sees state of this shirt.

DAVE   Ay, mine an' all. I think I'm more scared of facing her than the bloody police cavalry. What a mess!


## SCENE 9

**CHRISTINE and SANDRA are bathing BRIAN'S and RAY'S wounds.**

BRIAN   Ouch! Go bloody steady.

SANDRA   Shut up! Yer worse'n my arse wi' your moaning.

CHRISTINE   They're nowt but big babies, are men.

RAY   Hey up! Here we go! We've had seven bloody bells knocked out on us by the boys i' blue and we're not even allowed to flinch.

SANDRA   Well, it's right they're nobbut scratches.

BRIAN   Scratches nowt, them's bloody war wounds, is them – and they're painful, so go steady.

*Scene 9* **31**

CHRISTINE  Pain! You don't know the meaning of pain, you lot. I don't know what you'd do if you had to have kids.

SANDRA  It'd keep population down.

CHRISTINE  Ay, that's pain lad. There's no pain like childbirth.

RAY  What about having a size eleven police boot stamping on your bollocks?

SANDRA  Well, I wouldn't know about that, would I?

CHRISTINE  No, neither would he, Sandra . . . he hasn't any.

RAY  (*Looking down pants*) Ay, well, you might be right now, love.

CHRISTINE  Put 'em away and don't be so daft.

BRIAN  It's been a right bloody mullock today. It's done us no good at all, has this lot.

SANDRA  You can say that again. Press have had a field day. You've played right into their hands today.

RAY  It wasn't us. We turned up there for peaceful picketing. It were all them agitators and students what started trouble.

CHRISTINE  It were still you silly buggers what copped for it though, wasn't it?

RAY  Aye. Once it started, police just ran amok swinging at owt in range. It were barmy.

BRIAN  I don't mind telling you, it frightened me to death. Coppers were all over – jumping on cars and over walls – they even went in the houses after blokes.

CHRISTINE  And the cameras were there filming it all. They couldn't have set it up any better if they'd tried. It'll all be on the telly – 'Miners' riots' – they'll get some bloody mileage out of this, will the Government. And you silly sods played right up to 'em.

BRIAN  I tell you, it weren't our fault. It were them troublecausers.

32    *Black Roses*

SANDRA    It don't matter, that. Who can tell a bloody agitator from a right miner on the telly? You'll all be tarred wi' the same brush. If Union wants to get public support for us cause it's gonna have to get sorted out. They've done all this shouting about organising and having experience in this sort of thing. They make me laugh.

CHRISTINE    They've learnt nowt from the past. They've gone in like bulls in a china shop. They're gonna come unstuck, as sure as eggs is eggs. But will they listen? Will they hell. We've had that Jack Woodhead down at soup kitchen shouting his mouth off about women diluting the strike effort. We're there feeding twice as many women and children as there are pickets at Union kitchen and raising us own money, and that bugger dares to come round criticising.

SANDRA    Betty Sharp rounded on him right, last time he came down. 'Jack Woodhead' she says 'that's aptly named. You haven't a drop of sense in your entire body. How dare you come down here criticising us when you Union buggers couldn't organise a piss-up in a brewery. Now sod off or we'll stick yon wooden head of thine in the stewpot.'

RAY    He's alright, is Jack Woodhead. His heart's in the right place.

CHRISTINE    It's a shame his brain in't. Aye, he's a nice enough fella. It's just that he's got no idea. Local branch is just chasing its tail.

SANDRA    What do you expect? It's same at national level. Nobody gets on, allus falling out and getting in each other's way. It's not surprising they're making no progress – left hand don't know what right's doing.

CHRISTINE    What do you expect? They're only men.

BRIAN    Hey up! Here we go. Listen to the old German Gear get going.

RAY    German who?

*Scene 9* **33**

BRIAN    German Gear. She's one of them feminine liberationists.

RAY    Never heard of her.

CHRISTINE    I'm not surprised. He means Germaine Greer.

RAY    Oh! Is her husband a film star?

BRIAN    I've got no time for them feminists.

SANDRA    Hey up, I'm a feminist, buggerlugs.

BRIAN    Apart from our lass, I mean.

RAY    You're not, Sandra, are you?

SANDRA    Course I am.

RAY    What for?

SANDRA    What for? Because I've seen what a mess you blokes are making of the job and I'm sure women can do better.

BRIAN    Nay, lass. How?

SANDRA    I don't know, but we can't do no worse than you lot have. I think you must have seen off just about every scrap of public support we've ever had today.

BRIAN    Aye. Very good. You know what not to do but what would you actually *do*?

CHRISTINE    We ought to have some form of women's demonstration. Peaceful, like . . . just to show our unity and support for the cause.

SANDRA    That's a good idea. We could contact other support groups in Yorkshire and march in Sheffield, or summat.

CHRISTINE    Or even better, support groups all over the country, and march in London.

SANDRA    Aye, Downing Street.

CHRISTINE    That'd show 'em.

SANDRA    Aye, but nowt violent – peaceful protest to demonstrate us solidarity.

**34**  *Black Roses*

CHRISTINE   And let 'em put that on the telly. It'd be real if we could organise it. D'yer think we could?

SANDRA   I don't see why not. We could certainly do wi' a new approach and that might just be the answer.

BRIAN   It'll never come off . . . and any road, if it does, what good d'yer think it'll do?

RAY   Aye, nobody'll take no notice of a load of women tramping through London.

CHRISTINE   How do you know, Dopey?

SANDRA   Aye, what do you know about it? I mean Union lots done alright, haven't they? I don't think, if we tried, we could make a bigger cock-up than the Union has. I think we should have a go.

CHRISTINE   Me too. At least it'll show the public we're not all savages from pit villages. It'll show the human side of the struggle – how families is struggling together – unity and that. Yeah, let's do it.


**SCENE 10**

On the coach, all swaying and singing.

ALL   'Here we go' (*etc.*)

SANDRA   Hey, look at him there. He's got a lovely bum. 'Hello, darling.' (*Kiss kiss*)

CHRISTINE   Sandra, behave yourself.

SANDRA   Hey, he smiled at me. Ooh, I could live here if all the men are like that.

DOREEN   Look at him, there, he's got a handbag.

SANDRA   So what? All the men in London have handbags, it's fashion.

CHRISTINE   I can just see our Ray going down the club wi' one of mine.

*Scene 10*  **35**

DOREEN   Ooh aye, can you just see 'em all at Union meetings marching in with their handbags?

SANDRA   Aye, and hitting police with 'em on picket duty.

(**Another verse of 'Here we go'.**)

DOREEN   There's Post Office Tower. Look, it's huge.

CHRISTINE   Reminds me of our Ray. (*Women laugh and cheer.*)

SANDRA   You should be so lucky.

DOREEN   Does the end revolve as well? (*More raucous laughter from other women*)

CHRISTINE   Yeah, and light up.

(**They are getting hysterical. More singing of 'Here we go'.**)

BETTY SHARP   Right, girls, we're here. (*Cheers*) Arthur's dropping us off here, in the park. This is the rallying point for all the women's groups from all over the country. We're having speeches, and that, and then moving on to Downing Street. Now then, have a good time, enjoy yersen's but above all, don't forget what we're here for – a peaceful show of solidarity with us menfolk. So have a right good day and we'll meet back here at six p.m. Is that right, Arthur?

ARTHUR   Aye, love.

BETTY SHARP   Right, let's go then!

(**All cheer and form conga off bus. They sing these words to 'conga' tune.**)

ALL   We've come down here from Yorkshire,
We're marching down from Yorkshire,
   It's a fact you see,
   We'll fight the NCB
They're trying to starve us back now,
   'Cos money we don't have now,
   They won't succeed,
   We're a tough breed.
(*Singing continues muted as they all mingle.*)

36   *Black Roses*

WELSH WIFE    You're from Yorkshire then, is it?

CHRISTINE    We are that, flower – Barnsley – where are you from, then?

WELSH WIFE    Dowlais, lovey, in Wales. Been on the road since five, we have.

CHRISTINE    It's fantastic this, isn't it? I can't believe it.

WELSH WIFE    Dyu! I'd have never thought it could've been so successful. I tell you, girl, it makes me wanna weep. I just been talking to a girl from Kent who's palled up with another girl from Newcastle.

CHRISTINE    It's bloody brilliant, is this. What a show of solidarity. Thatcher can't ignore this – all women united.

WELSH WIFE    If somebody had said a year ago I'd be here today, doing what I am, I'd have thought they were soft in the head, I would.

CHRISTINE    I know, same here. I tell you what, my old man thinks I'm crazy, but I reckon seeing this lot would make him change his mind. Come on, love, join in.

**(They latch on to the conga line.)**

ALL    We've come down [up] here from Yorkshire [South Wales] (*etc.*)

BETTY SHARP    (*Speech*) Now then, girls, it's grand to see so many wives from all over the country gathered like this in such a show of solidarity. When news of this rally gets round, people – men – will start to take us seriously at last. They'll know we mean business. Back home we're fighting on two fronts – first and foremost against Coal Board and the pit closures and second against old-fashioned ideas of the Union, what just seem to be unable to grasp the fact that women are a force to be reckoned with. We're miners' wives. That don't mean we're simple, only that we aren't used to the phrases and words and ideas being bandied about in this strike. But this I promise you – we've had five months now on the

*Scene 10* **37**

picket lines and my political education is being gained at a gallop. I reckon in a year's time we'll be answering all the Union's questions and criticisms. (*All cheer.*) Come on then, girls, let's go and pay a call on Maggie.

ALL    (**All cheer, and march as they sing to the tune of 'It's a long way to Tipperary.'**)

It's a long way to come from Yorkshire,
It's a long way from home,
It's a long way to come from Yorkshire,
But it's a fact that's known,
They're trying to close our pits down,
And throw us on the dole,
It's a long way to come from Yorkshire,
But we'll fight for our coal.

MARGARET    I'm dying for a pee, Maureen. Where's toilets?

MAUREEN    You'll be lucky, lovey, they've all been locked up for the day.

MARGARET    You what?

MAUREEN    That's right, we asked a bobby early on. 'Toilets darling?' he says, 'You'll be lucky, they've all been closed today.' 'What for?' I says. 'Why do you think?' he says, 'So you lot'll be quicker getting back on your buses and going back home.'

MARGARET    The rotten sods. Well, they've had that, I'm staying till the very end if I've to march cross-legged.

MAUREEN    Me too. I might pop in to number ten and ask Maggie if I can use hers.

MARGARET    Good idea, Maureen. Come on.

ALL    (*Sing*) It's a long way to come from Yorkshire,
It's a long way from home,
It's a long way to come from Yorkshire,
But it's a fact that's known . . .

POLICE    That's far enough, ladies. I must advise you that access

38    *Black Roses*

INSPECTOR to Downing Street is not permitted, so you may as well just turn around and go back to your coaches.

BETTY SHARP You must be joking, old love. We've come all the way from Yorkshire to have a word with Maggie. You're not going to turn us back now, are you?

POLICE INSPECTOR I'm afraid so, ladies. The Prime Minister is not in residence at Downing Street at the moment so there really is no point in remaining here.

SANDRA Course she's in. She'll be hiding under the bed.

BETTY SHARP You're not going to get away with it that easy, flower.

POLICE INSPECTOR I would advise you not to try to cause any trouble. I have men standing by, should there be any attempt at disturbing the peace.

BETTY SHARP Don't worry, love. It's not agitators you're dealing with here. We're miners' wives an' we've more common than to start throwing us weight about, but I'll tell you summat, ducks, if we started, yon weedy twats wouldn't stand a chance! (*Women cheer.*) No, love, we've no intention of causing trouble. This here's a peaceful rally. We've done what we set out to do by getting everyone here. We've shown the Government and the people just what support there is for the miners and how united we are as women against pit closures . . . so you could have saved yourself a lot of bother, old mate. Worst you'll get from us is a minute's silence in respect for them miners, what's lost their lives on the picket line. And as for the old Iron Lady, here, take her this black rose and tell her it's a symbol of the death of the traditional mining communities and tell her there's hundreds of iron ladies up in Yorkshire what'll give her and her puppets a run for their money, eh girls?

(**More cheering, followed by soft humming of 'I am Woman,' as women parade, dropping black roses. Women walk round and sit down eating sandwiches.**)

MARGARET Do you want a sandwich, Maureen?

*Scene 10* **39**

MAUREEN No thanks, love, I'm alright. I've just had an apple.

MARGARET What about a cup of tea?

MAUREEN Oh you must be joking. I'm busting for a pee. Don't even talk about it.

DOREEN It were a right rotten trick, were that – locking all the bogs.

MARGARET Aye, I know. I'm busting an' all, but I'm not gonna let it spoil my day.

**(Enter two POLICEMEN.)**

POLICEMAN 1 Come on, ladies, keep moving please.

DOREEN Oh give up, copper, leave us alone. We're just resting us feet.

POLICEMAN 2 Not here, you're not. Now come on, get up and move on.

MAUREEN Aye up. I'm fed up of this lot. You're rotten bastards, you lot are. That were a sod's trick, locking all the bogs. Why don't you just leave us alone?

POLICEMAN 1 Well, darling, I tell you what . . . I'd hate you to think that we was unreasonable so look, here you go, here's an empty bottle for you to have a pee in.

MAUREEN Oh very funny, constable.

POLICEMAN 2 Well come on, you birds reckon you can do anything a man can. Let's see you pee in there without spilling.

DOREEN (*Wiggles little finger*) Well, I'm sure you wouldn't have any difficulty getting yours in there . . . big boy.

MAUREEN Why don't you lend us your helmet, constable, we could all pee in that.

MARGARET Aye . . . then you really would be a pisshead. (*Laughs*) (*Laughter from women.*)

POLICEMAN 1 Alright, that'll do now. Get moving before we take a few down to the station.

40    *Black Roses*

(**Women move away, laughing and grunting.**)

POLICEMAN 2    Bloody women.

ALL    They're trying to close our pits down
And throw us on the dole
(*Becoming quieter*)
It's a long way to come from Yorkshire
But we'll fight for our coal.

(**The women are back on the bus, tired but happy.**)

SANDRA    It's been fantastic, hasn't it?

CHRISTINE    Best day of my life.

SANDRA    All them other women there – come from all over the country.

CHRISTINE    And not a bit of trouble – organisation were spot on. You know, we've shown the country today that women's support groups are a force to be reckoned with.

DOREEN    Aye, it'll do the cause a power of good when people see us on the telly – no violence or bitterness, just unity.

SANDRA    And all the support we've had from people in the street. I mean I'd never thought that anybody in London would've been interested in what's happening in Yorkshire.

CHRISTINE    I know, but loads 'as said like 'Well done' and 'Good luck' to me.

MARGARET    And I've seen house wi' 'Coal not dole' stickers in the windows.

CHRISTINE    I tell you, it's really getting going, is this. It'll not be so long before Union starts to realise we've as much clout, if not more, than they have in this job.

DOREEN    Hey, I can't wait to get home and tell our Dave about this. I hope he got our Tracey's tea alright. Hey look . . . and I've got a bit of sun tan!

*Scene 11* **41**

SANDRA   What do you think the papers will make of us efforts today then, Betty?

BETTY SHARP   Not a right lot, love. It's all gone too well for them to be interested.

SANDRA   You know, before all this I just used to read papers and believe it were all gospel. I know better now . . . it's not fair.

BETTY SHARP   No, nowt's fair in life. I'm the same as you. All them things you just used to take for granted, I see them differently now.

SANDRA   Whatever happens now, things will never be the same for me . . . Is that a good thing, Betty?

BETTY SHARP   Yes, love, I think so . . . it's like growing up, isn't it . . . it's realising.

SANDRA   Yeah, sod the press, eh! We know we're right.


**SCENE 11**

BANK MANAGER, WELFARE LADY, SOCIAL SECURITY WORKER and SOCIAL WORKER are positioned around the stage. The bank manager is lit from above by a spotlight. The other three have similar spotlights, but these are not lit. During this scene, each time DOREEN approaches one of the other four characters that person's spotlight goes up, while that of the character she has just left is faded. Doreen wanders in overwhelmed, as if in a cathedral. She approaches the bank manager.

DOREEN   Good morning.

BANK MANAGER   Good morning. Can I help you?

DOREEN   Yes, I've come about my mortgage.

BANK MANAGER   Ah yes. Good. How can I help?

42 *Black Roses*

DOREEN | Well, I don't think I can pay it.

BANK MANAGER | (*Hardening*) I see.

DOREEN | My husband's a miner.

BANK MANAGER | I see.

DOREEN | And so we've hardly any money coming in.

BANK MANAGER | I see.

WELFARE LADY | Next.

WELFARE LADY | Name?

DOREEN | Doreen Lockwood.

WELFARE LADY | Address?

DOREEN | 27 Ashenhurst Avenue, Cridlington.

WELFARE LADY | Dependants?

DOREEN | What?

WELFARE LADY | Dependants. Who depends on you? Who do you support? Children?

DOREEN | Oh yes, two . . . Tracey and Ian.

WELFARE LADY | Ages?

DOREEN | Nine and fourteen.

SOCIAL SECURITY WORKER | Next. What is your social security number?

DOREEN | YS 200148

*Scene 11* **43**

| | |
|---|---|
| SOCIAL SECURITY WORKER | Are you currently in employment? |
| DOREEN | Yes, part-time, three afternoons a week. |
| SOCIAL SECURITY WORKER | What are your weekly earnings? |
| DOREEN | Eighteen pounds. |
| SOCIAL SECURITY WORKER | Husband's name? |
| DOREEN | David. |
| SOCIAL SECURITY WORKER | Occupation? |
| DOREEN | Miner. |
| SOCIAL SECURITY WORKER | I see. |
| SOCIAL WORKER | Mrs Lockwood? I'm so pleased you could call. Now how can I help? |
| DOREEN | Well, you see my husband's a miner. |
| SOCIAL WORKER | Oh, right. |
| DOREEN | And with him being on strike, we're a bit short. |
| SOCIAL WORKER | Right. |
| DOREEN | And I'm finding it very difficult making ends meet. |
| SOCIAL WORKER | Oh, right. |
| DOREEN | I just wondered if you could help? |

**44**  *Black Roses*

| | |
|---|---|
| SOCIAL WORKER | Right. |
| WELFARE LADY | Requirements? |
| DOREEN | Er? |
| WELFARE LADY | What are the children's requirements? |
| DOREEN | Well, new clothes really, for school. |
| WELFARE LADY | What in particular? |
| DOREEN | Well Tracey could do with a skirt and jumper and Ian some new trousers and a jumper and both could use some new shoes. |
| WELFARE LADY | That's rather a large demand, Mrs Lockwood . . . |
| BANK MANAGER | Rather a large demand. |
| DOREEN | But what else can we do? We've no money coming in. |
| BANK MANAGER | But to suspend payment altogether, Mrs Lockwood, for how long? |
| DOREEN | Well, I can't say. Perhaps a month or two, I can't say. |
| BANK MANAGER | And therein lies the problem, Mrs Lockwood . . . you can't say. |
| SOCIAL SECURITY WORKER | And what is the total income of the household per week? |
| DOREEN | Well it's very difficult to say just now. |
| SOCIAL SECURITY WORKER | Why is that? |
| DOREEN | Well it varies so much week to week, but it's not a lot. |

SCENE *Scene 11* **45**

| | |
|---|---|
| SOCIAL SECURITY WORKER | That's not good enough, Mrs Lockwood, I need to know exactly. |
| SOCIAL WORKER | Exactly what do you want, Mrs Lockwood? |
| DOREEN | Well, just any help you can give. |
| SOCIAL WORKER | Do you mean financial or supportive? |
| DOREEN | Well both, really. |
| WELFARE LADY | Both? Well you are allowed a grant for both, Mrs Lockwood, but the grant differs because of their ages. Your daughter is allowed a grant of £9 and your son £6 – he's under eleven, you see. |
| DOREEN | Is that all? |
| BANK MANAGER | Yes, Mrs Lockwood, that is all, I'm afraid. What did you expect? |
| DOREEN | Well . . . I just thought that perhaps you could just work out the time we don't pay now and add it on to the end of the twenty years. |
| BANK MANAGER | Oh no, Mrs Lockwood, it doesn't work like that at all. |
| SOCIAL SECURITY WORKER | He doesn't work at all, you say, but does he have any income? |
| DOREEN | Well, he gets £1 a day for picket duty. |
| SOCIAL SECURITY WORKER | No strike pay? |
| DOREEN | No, only that, and only when he goes picketing. |
| SOCIAL SECURITY WORKER | Are you sure? |

46    *Black Roses*

| | |
|---|---|
| WELFARE LADY | Are you sure? |
| DOREEN | Yes. |
| WELFARE LADY | It's just that size ten is very popular and I don't know if we've much left. |
| DOREEN | Well, what about trousers? She can wear trousers and with winter coming on . . . |
| SOCIAL WORKER | Things will get more difficult – heating and lighting bills will go up, you'll need more clothing – it's always more expensive in the winter. |
| DOREEN | I know. I don't know where the money will come from. |
| BANK MANAGER | Well, we can probably help a little there, Mrs Lockwood. I have permission to offer you a loan facility to tide you over this difficult period and to enable you to keep up with your mortgage payments. |
| DOREEN | How much? |
| SOCIAL SECURITY WORKER | £29.40 per week, Mrs Lockwood, less your earnings and your husband's picketing money . . . that's £6.40. |
| DOREEN | Is that all? |
| WELFARE LADY | Yes, I told you, it's a very popular size. These are the only pair we have. |
| DOREEN | But they're so old-fashioned. How long have you had them in? Nobody wears flares anymore. |
| WELFARE LADY | We're not concerned with fashion, Mrs Lockwood. We're concerned with practical help. |
| SOCIAL WORKER | So what practical help can I offer, Mrs Lockwood? |
| DOREEN | Just tell me what I can do to make ends meet. I just feel so helpless. Things are just going from bad to worse. |
| BANK MANAGER | Things will get worse, Mrs Lockwood. You should consider a loan. |

*Scene 11* **47**

DOREEN But how will I pay it back?

BANK All that can be organised when the strike is over.
MANAGER

DOREEN But doesn't that mean I'll be paying a mortgage and a loan off together, plus interest on both?

BANK Yes, that's correct, Mrs Lockwood.
MANAGER

DOREEN And you think that's a help?

WELFARE They're better than nothing, Mrs Lockwood.
LADY

DOREEN Not for Tracey, they're not.

WELFARE Well, to be perfectly frank, Mrs Lockwood, the answer
LADY to that is in your hands.

DOREEN What do you mean?

WELFARE You have a choice, Mrs Lockwood. You don't have to
LADY rely on welfare.

SOCIAL Take it or leave it, Mrs Lockwood, I'm afraid that's how
SECURITY it works out.
WORKER

DOREEN But it's a pittance. I can't manage on that.

SOCIAL Well, the answer to that is simple, Mrs Lockwood.
SECURITY
WORKER

DOREEN What can I do?

DOREEN (*To social worker*) What *can* I do?

SOCIAL Well, you've made the most of all that the benefits and
WORKER welfare system can offer. If you can't manage on that, Mrs Lockwood, then there's only one solution.

DOREEN That is not a solution.

BANK It's the best I can do, Mrs Lockwood. I'm sorry!
MANAGER

48    *Black Roses*

(At every change now a bell rings. DOREEN goes from one to another like a pinball machine. As each character says 'I'm sorry', they put a 'faceless mask' in front of them. The coloured lights flash on and off haphazardly.

SOCIAL SECURITY WORKER   That is the maximum weekly payout available to you at the moment. I'm sorry!

SOCIAL WORKER   I can only offer help within the limitations of the various departments, Mrs Lockwood. I'm sorry!

WELFARE LADY   One pair black trousers, one pair grey socks and that's your grant gone, Mrs Lockwood. I'm sorry!

BANK MANAGER   We are not a charitable institution, Mrs Lockwood.

SOCIAL WORKER   You could earn more money.

WELFARE LADY   You're not in a position to complain.

SOCIAL WORKER   That's all I can do.

(Confusion mounts.)

BANK MANAGER   At the end of the day our books must balance.

SOCIAL SECURITY WORKER   There are a lot worse off than you.

WELFARE LADY   Every little helps.

SOCIAL WORKER   You'll adjust in time.

BANK MANAGER   Won't your husband consider going back?

| | |
|---|---|
| SOCIAL SECURITY WORKER | Try to persuade him. |
| WELFARE LADY | There's no future in it. |
| SOCIAL WORKER | Think of the children. |
| BANK MANAGER | Things will get more difficult. |
| SOCIAL SECURITY WORKER | It could be ended so easily. |
| WELFARE LADY | It's not worth it. |
| SOCIAL WORKER | You can't go on. |
| BANK MANAGER | You could lose everything. |
| SOCIAL SECURITY WORKER | It's an impossible struggle. |
| WELFARE LADY | The odds are against you. |
| SOCIAL WORKER | You haven't a chance. |
| BANK MANAGER | Get out while you can. |
| SOCIAL SECURITY WORKER | Go back. |
| WELFARE LADY | Give up. |

50    *Black Roses*

SOCIAL WORKER  Go back.

ALL  Go back, Mrs Lockwood, it's all you can do. Give it all up and go Back, go Back, go Back. (*Echo and fade*)

**SCENE 12**

DOREEN is left alone on the stage after Scene 11. She is distressed and clutching a plastic bag containing the flares. She is wiping her eyes and composing herself as TRACEY enters.

TRACEY  Hi, Mam.

DOREEN  Hello, Tracey love. (*Covering up*)

TRACEY  Are you alright?

DOREEN  Yes thanks, love . . . are you?

TRACEY  Yeah, fine.

DOREEN  I've been to the welfare to get you some new school trousers today, love.

TRACEY  Aw thanks, Mam.

(TRACEY takes trousers out of the bag. She sees that they are flares.)

DOREEN  I'm sorry, love.

(We see in TRACEY'S face the inner struggle brought on by the situation. There is a long electric pause. Eventually Tracey turns and says brightly, but with a catch in her voice . . .)

TRACEY  Thanks, Mam.

(Pause. They hug each other tightly, and exit.)

**SCENE 13**

BRIAN, SANDRA, RICHARD and KIRSTY WOOD, and REPORTERS 1–3.

REPORTER 1  You've been on strike nine months now, Mr Wood. How are you and your family coping?

*Scene 13* **51**

BRIAN   Well, I can't say it's not been hard – bloody hard – but there have been some compensations.

REPORTER 2   It's been hard . . .

REPORTER 3   . . . bloody hard.

REPORTER 2   What about you, Mrs Wood?

SANDRA   Well, despite the difficulties, I think it's brought us together as a family and a community.

REPORTER 3   And these difficulties. Could you be more specific?

SANDRA   Well, same as everybody else . . . difficulties brought about by having no money coming in . . . but we're all in the same boat and we've helped one another out.

REPORTER 2   No money coming in.

REPORTER 1   Obviously financial difficulties are at the forefront of your mind. How are you feeling now Christmas is drawing closer?

BRIAN   Well, it won't be the same as it's been. Again though, that don't mean it'll be worse . . . just different.

REPORTER 2   Things won't be the same . . .

REPORTER 3   . . . again.

REPORTER 2   So the approach of Christmas brings with it no joy?

SANDRA   Well no, not joy exactly, but we're not going to do too badly.

REPORTER 3   No joy this Christmas for miners and their families.

REPORTER 1   What about you, young man? What would you like for Christmas? A computer?

RICHARD   Yeah!

REPORTER 2   And what are his chances of getting what he wants, Mr Wood?

MR WOOD   Well, he's no chance of getting a computer, has he, but he knows that.

**52** *Black Roses*

REPORTER 1    Christmas of disappointment for miners' kids.

REPORTER 3    (*To daughter*) Will you be going to lots of parties and discos, young lady?

KIRSTY    No.

REPORTER 2    Does that make you upset or cross?

KIRSTY    No.

REPORTER 3    Do you feel you're missing out?

KIRSTY    No.

REPORTER 1    Won't you be disappointed when your friends are going?

KIRSTY    My friends won't be going either.

REPORTER 3    The teenage Cinderellas of the coalfields.

SANDRA    Look, we haven't a lot of spare cash for Christmas, but that doesn't mean we'll have a miserable time.

REPORTER 2    No cash for Christmas.

REPORTER 1    A miserable time.

SANDRA    There won't be the presents there were last year.

REPORTER 3    No presents this year.

SANDRA    But that's not the point.

REPORTER 2    There's no point.

SANDRA    The point is that out of all this hardship . . .

REPORTER 1    Hardship.

SANDRA    . . . there's sprung a real feeling of togetherness. It doesn't matter that financially it's a lean time.

REPORTER 3    It's a lean time.

SANDRA    What matters is the unity in the community and the family. We're pulling each other through. The disappointment . . .

Scene 14   **53**

| | |
|---|---|
| REPORTER 2 | Disappointment. |
| SANDRA | . . . difficulties . . . |
| REPORTER 1 | Difficulties . . . |
| SANDRA | . . . and upsets . . . |
| REPORTER 3 | Upsets. |
| SANDRA | . . . just bind us closer together. We know each other and respect each other like we've never done before. Out of all this mess there's sprung something that means more than all the turkeys, mince pies, discos and computers in the world. There's a real feeling of love and isn't that what it should all be about, eh? I'll tell you something, despite everything this is going to be the best Christmas any of us have ever had. We'll see to that, don't you worry. |

(**REPORTERS** look disappointed.)

## SCENE 14

Band plays medley of 'merry' Christmas carols and songs, starting with 'Deck the Halls' 'Jingle Bells', 'Rudolph', 'White Christmas', etc. The effect to be created is one of joyful chaotic hustle and bustle. Movement and dance involving paper chains, table decorations, Christmas tree. All sing along with the band.

| | |
|---|---|
| SANDRA | Where have all the decorations come from? |
| CHRISTINE | George Bright's newsagents . . . he's donated 'em all. |
| SANDRA | Brilliant. |
| DOREEN | What about the tree? |
| CHRISTINE | Moorhouses farm. |
| MARGARET | Cridlington Co-op have given us fifty loaves. |
| SANDRA | Has Chippy Booth given us two fish, then? |
| MARGARET | Morelli's supplied ice cream for nowt. |

54   *Black Roses*

CHRISTINE   Surprising what a bit of cheek'll do, eh?

SANDRA   You're not kidding.

**(All is ready. They look around.)**

CHRISTINE   Right let 'em in.

**(Cast enter as excited kids.)**

SANDRA   Right, sit down . . . Keep quiet . . . Listen . . . Oh bugger it, get on and enjoy yourselves.

**(The band continues to play. 'Audience' sings.)**

CHRISTINE   And now, for your entertainment . . . the magnificent Marvo!

**(MAGICIAN enters, does simple tricks. Cheers and laughter from audience.)**

CHRISTINE   And now, for your further entertainment . . . our very own Jackie Clayton.

*(Shouts and jeers for Jackie.)*

JACKIE   Now then, are you all having a good time?

ALL   YES.

JACKIE   Good lot. Now then . . . what's this?

**(He raises thumb and first two fingers and wiggles them.)**

Sooty in the nude. *(Jeers from the audience.)* It's the way I tell 'em, me old flowers . . . that's what sets me apart from the rest. Hey up, hey up, have you heard this one? There were these two dogs and one says to the other, 'Have you done yer pools', and the other one says, 'Yeah, but I missed the post'. *(Jeers from the audience.)* Do you want more, or do you give in?

ALL   *(Loudly)* We give in.

JACKIE   Right, you miserable so-and-so's, I'll love yer and leave yer just for now. *(Cheers)* But before I go *(Groans)* I'll introduce a lass you'll all know. She's a bit nervous like, but she's gonna sing a song what she's written herself. I'm sure you'll all enjoy it, so I want you to give a right warm welcome to Tracey Lockwood.

(Cheers as TRACEY gets up very nervously. She sings to the tune of 'Amazing Grace'. As the song proceeds, the audience, visibly moved, calm down.)

For many months we've struggled hard,
And now the pit's a part
Of all our lives and history,
The centre of my heart.

As time goes on and things get hard,
I know we will pull through,
And years from now our sons will mine,
And it's all thanks to you.

It's taken time to build our lives,
Our strong community,
But strength and love will see us through,
To keep unity.

(When she has finished there is a pause and then the clapping starts, slowly building up as people compose themselves.)

SANDRA  Thanks, Tracey, that were fantastic. You ought to stick at song writing. If that's owt to go by you could have a big future. And I'd like to thank Darren and the lads in the band for coming along and playing for us. (*Cheers from all.*) And now for the moment you've all been waiting for. We've been out by the door listening and just as Tracey were finishing we heard bells jingling. So if the band'll play for us, we'll all sing 'Jingle Bells' and welcome Father Christmas in.

(Band and singing. Enter FATHER CHRISTMAS. All rush to him. There is chaos. The band gradually fades, as do the lights. A muted cornet plays 'In the Bleak Midwinter'. A blue spotlight comes up near the front. SANDRA breaks away from the now muted action around Father Christmas and comes into the blue spotlight. CHRISTINE notices and goes down to her.)

**56** *Black Roses*

CHRISTINE   It's been fantastic, hasn't it?

SANDRA   Yeah.

CHRISTINE   Best Christmas I've ever had. I'd have never believed it if you'd said a couple of month ago.

SANDRA   No, I know.

CHRISTINE   The build-up and that, the support . . . brilliant.

SANDRA   Yeah.

CHRISTINE   Hey, come on, Sandra love. Don't let it get to you.

SANDRA   It's just so . . . I don't know . . . temporary. You know what I mean.

CHRISTINE   Aye, I do, love. I know exactly what you mean. That's why it's so important you make the most of it now, while you've chance.

SANDRA   It's all very well that, but what about tomorrow, next week, next month?

CHRISTINE   They'll come soon enough. If there's one thing I've learnt out of this job, it's that you've to live for the moment. It's no good allus brooding about what's gonna happen.

SANDRA   I know, but how can you enjoy yourself wi' all this hanging over us.

CHRISTINE   It's hard, but we've got to or else they'll grind us down. Hey, do you know what I've done this time?

SANDRA   What?

CHRISTINE   I ordered our Ray, Kath and Andrew a right nice present each out of the catalogue, delivered last week. You should've seen their faces this morning. It were great. They still don't know how I did it.

SANDRA   How did you do it?

CHRISTINE   Simple. I just ordered 'em. By time I have to pay the instalments it might be all over.

|  |  |
|---|---|
| SANDRA | It might not be. How d'yer know? |
| CHRISTINE | I don't, and what's more I don't care. |
| SANDRA | You're crackers. |
| CHRISTINE | I know, but it's same as I say, you've to live for the minute. Forget about what it's gonna be like in January and February. We've a bloody good party going on in there, the like of which hasn't been seen in this village afore – and this is just a start – there's lots more to look forward to. So come on, let's get in and enjoy us bloody selves. We can be miserable tomorrow. |
| SANDRA | I am strong, I am invincible, eh? |
| CHRISTINE | I am Woman. C'mon kid. |

**(Cornet echoes phrase from 'I am Woman'.)**

## SCENE 15

**Home scene. RAY is folding clothes. Enter CHRISTINE.**

|  |  |
|---|---|
| CHRISTINE | Hello, love. Oh have you done that ironing? Bless you, love. I'm sorry I'm late, we've had a right rush on today. Some clothing parcels have come in from Belgium. |
| RAY | Have they? (*Miserable*) |
| CHRISTINE | What's up, love? You look fed up. |
| RAY | I am. |
| CHRISTINE | Why? |
| RAY | Why? Bloody hell, Chris . . . look around. Why do you think? |
| CHRISTINE | You haven't let it get you down, Ray? I know it's hard, but we're managing. We've got into a routine and it's working. |
| RAY | No it's not, Chris . . . it's a shambles. We've struggled to get this far and it's been hard – nearly a year – and if we |

58  *Black Roses*

were to go back to work tomorrow it'd be another two or three year before things are right again.

CHRISTINE   But we'll win, Ray, I know we will. We get strength from us unity. We'll beat 'em and go back with us heads held high.

RAY   That's bloody rubbish, Christine. Don't you read your papers? I do, all bloody day . . . and sit watching telly. We've had it . . . strike's broken . . . it's all over, bar the shouting.

CHRISTINE   Don't talk like that, Ray. A few scabs have crawled back and the press is blaring it all out of proportion. You step out into that street and ask folk there if strike's broken – they'll tell you.

RAY   Look at us though, Chris . . . scratching by on thirty quid a week . . . can't pay the mortgage . . . We're going to have to sell this house before long. Then what? Kids have no decent clothes, we hardly eat, we're bloody frozen 'cos we can't afford heating, we can't go out at night. Soon we're gonna have to stop watching the telly 'cos we can't afford electricity. What's happening to us, Chris?

CHRISTINE   What's happening, Ray, is that we're fighting for us right to work and us children's right to work and we've to keep that at front of us minds because everything else is unimportant – just detail.

RAY   That's crap, Chris. Look around. Look what we're doing to usselves. We've no bloody chance. We're flogging a dead horse. We're beaten, crushed.

CHRISTINE   Don't be pathetic. We've struggled for nearly a year now. I'd never have believed it could've been done, but we've done it. I can't believe we can do it for another year, but we will if we have to, and another year after that. Course it's easier in the short term to give in, but I tell you, we'd be regretting it within a month. We've built up strength and unity over this year, we can't just let that all go.

| | |
|---|---|
| RAY | Strength and unity . . . I'm sick of hearing about strength and bloody unity. Strength and unity aren't bloody feeding us, are they? |
| CHRISTINE | Yes they bloody are, my lad. Strength and unity is all that's feeding us. The bleeding Welfare State certainly isn't. It's strength and unity that's making donations, growing and pooling vegetables from allotments, making dinners in the soup kitchens, parties for the kids. All that's strength and unity and it's proper strength and unity, from the heart, not the bullshit Union 'United we Stand' crap that's crumbling before their eyes. This is for real. |
| RAY | You're getting clever at making speeches. |
| CHRISTINE | Well, I understand more now, Ray. Time was when I didn't know and I didn't want to know about that sort of thing. But I'm involved now and being more involved has made me more aware. |
| RAY | Don't I know it. |
| CHRISTINE | What does that mean? |
| RAY | Well, the bloody women's support group . . . it's all we ever hear these days. I'm sick of it . . . it's doing you no good . . . it's . . . it's made you different. |
| CHRISTINE | It has that, Ray. It's made us all different. It's made us realise what we are, what we're capable of. Up till now we've just drifted along, but now, given a bit of direction and a cause what's worth fighting for we've found a purpose. Look at us now, talking about politics. We'd never have done this a year ago. Life were all ale and skittles – me doing the housework, you going to work. That's all changed now, Ray, and me for one, I'm glad. Things won't be the same again. Ray, things is going to be different . . . and better. |
| RAY | Aye . . . Well . . . happen then this isn't best time to say what I were going to . . . |
| CHRISTINE | What? |

**60** *Black Roses*

RAY     Well . . . some of the lads reckon the strike's about to fold so some on us are thinking of getting together and going back.

CHRISTINE     You what?

RAY     I said I'm thinking of going back.

CHRISTINE     You're bloody joking Ray . . . You? Scabbing?

RAY     Going back to work . . . for yours and kids' sake.

CHRISTINE     Scabbing, Ray, bloody scabbing. Don't try to glorify it.

RAY     It's just common bloody sense, Christine. I'm finished. It's all that's left.

CHRISTINE     That's crap, Ray. It's not all that's left and you know it. I can't believe it . . . my own husband . . . a scab . . .

(She picks up a piece of paper.)

Look here. 'After God had finished the rattlesnake, the toad and vampire he had some awful substance left with which he made a scab. Where others have a heart, a scab carries a tumour of rotten principles. When a scab comes down the street men turn their backs, the angels weep in heaven and the Devil shuts the gates of Hell to keep him out.' Is that you, Ray . . . eh?

RAY     (*Snatches paper*) This is what I'm sick of . . . words . . . bravado. It were alright in the beginning when we might have had a chance, but not now . . . it's all gone empty and meaningless. It's as though we've been pushing usselves up a ladder all year and we've never noticed Government cutting rungs out from under us. Only way back now is to fall. I'm at end of the ladder, love.

CHRISTINE     Come on, Ray, you're just down, that's all. Things'll come right.

RAY     I can't take no more. I look at you and the kids and I think enough's enough. You mean more to me than the Union and the lads I work with. It's a matter of getting your priorities into perspective. I've given a lot to the Union. I must put family first now.

CHRISTINE  But going back won't make things easier for us, Ray. It'll be more difficult.

RAY  It will at first, I know, but things'll soon blow over. Someone has to make a move, love.

CHRISTINE  But why you, Ray?

RAY  I've had enough . . .

CHRISTINE  They've broken you.

RAY  If you like. But I'll tell you, deciding to go back were the hardest thing I've done all year.

CHRISTINE  Yes . . . you're gonna need some strength to go through wi' it.

RAY  I know that, love . . . but . . . well, I'm not the only one. There's a lot of blokes going, and thinking of going. It's only a matter of time, now.

CHRISTINE  So it's all over . . . all this and we've lost . . . I'm sick, Ray, I can't pretend I'm not. For a year I've fought bloody hard for a cause I still believe in Ray . . . a cause I'd fight on for . . . but . . . you're right . . . family comes first . . . for better or for worse, eh? . . . You do what you think fit, Ray . . . I'll back you up.

RAY  Thanks, love.


## SCENE 16

**Support group activity.**

SANDRA  There's another load of clothes parcels arrived at the Union rooms.

MARGARET  Where from?

SANDRA  Belgium again, I think.

MARGARET  It's marvellous, isn't it, where all the support comes from.

62    *Black Roses*

MAUREEN   I know, it's real. It's just a shame it's all to go to the Union.

SANDRA   Yeah, but there's nowt we can do about that. They're 'official' and we're not.

MARGARET   They're pillocks and we're not. It makes me poorly. Betty Sharp asked if she could address a branch meeting to report on the progress made by the women's support group and the secretary turned her down . . . said it wasn't the time or place.

MAUREEN   They won't recognise us at all. They're still thinking in terms of washing-up and that.

SANDRA   Someone were telling me they'd had some clothes in from France and Union had sat on 'em for long enough doing nowt and telling the women they'd sort it out. Now the women have gone in, they can't find hide nor hair of the parcels.

MARGARET   I tell you, they're frightened now. They know we're on top of 'em. We're better organised now than they ever will be.

**(Enter BETTY.)**

BETTY SHARP   Alright, everybody?

ALL   Hiya, Betty . . . (*etc.*)

BETTY SHARP   How we doing?

SANDRA   Great, we were just saying how much better organised we are than the Union.

BETTY SHARP   By bloody hell you can say that again. I'm pig sick of them prats down there. I'll swing for that Jack Woodhead before this job's over. I've just been down to see him about distributing clothing parcels. He's got a half-cocked idea about just taking 'em down to the pickets and letting 'em just dip in. I told him it should be properly organised. Leave it to us, I said. He says he's not having women telling him what to do – he'll deal with it. The prat!

*Scene 16* **63**

MARGARET They haven't a clue. They get down in that club supping on an evening . . .

SANDRA That's another thing. Where do they get money for all that?

MAUREEN I don't know. Summat's wrong somewhere.

MARGARET I think they're keeping their heads down now there's talk about going back.

BETTY SHARP Aye, that's another thing. They ought to be out there getting round the membership, scotching any idea about going back. But they're not, they're sitting about on their fat arses, grumbling about scabs drifting back.

SANDRA They'd have just been same if they'd been on the Titanic when it went down – sitting supping in the bar, complaining about lack of lifeboats.

MARGARET Icebergs crossing lines of demarcation.

MAUREEN Women and children first.

SANDRA And they wouldn't shut up till their heads went under.

MARGARET What makes you think that'd stop 'em?

MAUREEN They'd be forming picket lines outside Davy Jones' locker.

MARGARET They are prats.

**(Enter CHRISTINE, miserably.)**

SANDRA Hey up, Chris. What's up?

MARGARET Lost half a crown an' found sixpence?

CHRISTINE It's worse than that.

MAUREEN You're not pregnant? (*They laugh.*)

CHRISTINE No . . . our Ray's going back to work.

SANDRA Oh no, Chris.

CHRISTINE Yeah . . . I've tried my best to talk him out of it, but he's made his mind up. He's going next week.

**64** *Black Roses*

MARGARET Oh, Chris.

CHRISTINE (*Breaks down*) I'm so sorry . . . I tried . . . I really
did . . . I'm sorry.

MAUREEN It's alright Chris love. It's not your fault . . . come on,
love . . . cheer up.

MARGARET Aye, come on, give us a hand here . . . take your mind
off it . . . eh?

BETTY SHARP No.

MARGARET What?

BETTY SHARP I said no. If her husband's going back, then there's no
place for her here.

MARGARET I don't believe it.

MAUREEN What you saying Betty?

BETTY SHARP I'm saying, if her husband's going back, she can't work
here.

MAUREEN Bloody hell, Betty. Don't be such a bitch. Can't you see
she's upset enough?

BETTY SHARP Aye, she should be . . . and there's no way we're having
scabs' wives working here.

MARGARET Betty, she's worked here since day one. She's been one
of us, shoulder to shoulder. Have a bit of bloody
humanity. She's given us her support, she needs ours now.

BETTY SHARP No. If he goes back, she goes out of that door.

MAUREEN Bloody hell, Betty . . .

CHRISTINE It's alright, Maureen . . . don't . . . I knew I couldn't
work here no more . . . it don't matter . . . I'm sorry, but
I have to stick wi' me husband . . . I'll see yer around . . .
Good luck.

**(She exits. There is a long pause.)**

MARGARET Christ, I don't believe this, Betty. All the bloody time
we've spent getting things together, all united and

*Scene 16* **65**

organised and then just to blow one of us most loyal members out, just like that. It's just stupid.

MAUREEN It were a bit hard that, Betty. That poor woman's given her all this year.

BETTY SHARP It makes no difference, that. If her husband scabs, she's out.

MARGARET But it's her husband what's scabbing, not her. What's happened to all this 'I am Woman' business? We spend all this time shaking the shackles off and first opportunity you get, you slap 'em back on.

BETTY SHARP What do you mean?

MARGARET I thought we were free of them. I thought we'd won our independence . . . but you've just cut us own throats.

BETTY SHARP How's that?

MARGARET You condemned that woman on the actions of her husband, even though she's dead against him going back. You've let men split us ranks. All that unity and strength . . . It'll all break up if you carry on like this Betty . . .

SANDRA No it won't . . . Betty's right.

MAUREEN How come?

SANDRA Well, we just can't have Chris here if her husband's scabbing. Can't you see? It'll cause too much rankle. There'll be bad feeling and it'll break unity.

BETTY SHARP That's right. And another thing, it's not me what's broken us unity, it's Chris. I wasn't judging her on husband's actions, I were judging her on her own. She made a choice. It were her decision and she decided to go wi' her husband. It's her that's turned her back on us. She's a weak link. It's alright saying she's stood wi' us but she hasn't now, and it's now what really counts.

MAUREEN What could she do, Betty, if her husband said he were going back?

**66**  *Black Roses*

BETTY SHARP  She could have left him. If what she's been doing had really meant something, she'd have packed up and left him to it.

MARGARET  Bloody hell, Betty, that's a bit hard.

BETTY SHARP  It's a hard world, love. She's been playing at this game. When the chips were down, she had to go with him. That means she needs him more than she needs us . . . so she's no great loss, is she?

SANDRA  Betty's right. If us struggle's gonna be worth owt, we've to see it right through to the end . . . otherwise it's all back to square one. (*Pause*)

MARGARET  I just hope our Bob don't come round and say he's going back, that's all.

MAUREEN  (*Thoughtfully*) Aye.

**(Enter DOREEN, agitated.)**

DOREEN  Have you heard the news?

ALL  What? What news? (*etc.*)

DOREEN  Jack Woodhead's just been round to the club. It's official. He's had it from National Executive level, so it's right and there's nowt we can do about it . . . I can't believe it . . . twelve months' bloody hardship . . .

SANDRA  What's happened, Doreen?

DOREEN  It's over . . . strike's over. They've given in an' all the men have been told they've to report back to work tomorrow.

BETTY SHARP  Frigging hell. (*Long pause*)

DOREEN  It's dreadful. In the club they're as sick as parrots. There's blokes bawling their bloody eyes out down there.

BETTY SHARP  (*Quietly*) I'm not surprised . . . all this . . . all what we've done, worked for . . . all for bloody nothing. The miserable soft bastards.

*Scene 16* **67**

MARGARET   Come on, Betty. There's nowt we can do. It's out of our hands now.

MAUREEN   We can't all leave us husbands, Betty. (*She gets a look.*) Sorry.

SANDRA   What we gonna do . . . all this what we've built up . . . does it mean we're gonna lose everything?

BETTY SHARP   Does it chuff . . . we've only just started.

MARGARET   But Betty, it's no good now . . . us cause has finished . . . there's nowt left to fight for . . .

BETTY SHARP   Rubbish! It's all to fight for. We've been fighting on two fronts. That's been good in one way, 'cos strike's given us a focus to get ussens together. Well, that's gone now . . . but that don't mean we just give up . . . not bloody likely . . . it means we concentrate us efforts on usselves as women. The last thing we do now is just let usselves drop back into what we were. We've got brains and experience to build on and summat else we've got is respect of the men. I know there'll always be some pillocks who think a woman's place is in the kitchen but there's a lot now who know things won't be the same again. We've to capitalise on this now . . . it's up to us . . . together. (*They all hold hands.*) Now then . . . at least them as stuck strike out will be going back with their heads held up. So I say we go down and cheer 'em back in one last show of solidarity with 'em. What do you say, girls?

ALL   Yes. Aye . . . (*etc.*)

(**Band strike up 'Men of Harlech'. Women gather and unfurl banner. The women cheer and shout encouragement as imaginary procession files past. Then band stands and marches past and towards exit. Music fades. The excitement dies down. The women sit, the banner droops . . .**)

SANDRA   I just feel empty . . . drained . . . there's nothing left.

CHRISTINE   I know . . . a whole year and nothing to show.

68  *Black Roses*

DOREEN    No. There is a lot to show. Betty were right
          yesterday . . . we're united, we've solidarity, we've
          respect.

SANDRA    Yeah . . . we're women and we're proud.

          **(Cornet begins softly 'I am Woman'.)**

ALL       I am Woman, watch me grow
          See me standing toe to toe
          As I spread my loving arms across the land
          But I am still an embryo
          With a long long way to go
          Until I make my brother understand.

          Oh yes, I am wise but it's wisdom born of pain
          Yes I've paid the price
          But look how much I gained
          If I have to, I can do anything
          I am strong
          I am invincible
          I am Woman.

          **(Curtain.)**

# WRITING THE PLAY

*Black Roses* is based on the actual experiences of a group of miners' wives in Woolley, Yorkshire. Basing a play on real-life experiences gives the playwright several advantages, chiefly that the story-line, situations and even some of the characters are provided for you – all you have to do is find the dialogue which will shape everything into an effective theatrical piece.

In researching *Black Roses* I selected six short anecdotes from the many I heard. These formed the bones of the play. I had to build on them, often by providing beginnings or endings. The six incidents were:

- starting the kitchen and the rice pudding blowing up:

- the Orgreave riot;

- the financial trouble with mortgages and welfare

- the London trip;

- the Christmas party;

- going back.

Apart from these specific stories I picked up 'feelings' from the women of Woolley. These feelings included a sense of community and family strength, an appreciation of many things previously taken for granted, a mistrust of the press. All these 'feelings' I tried to include in the course of the play.

Having been given the skeleton of the play it was my job to flesh it out with dialogue. I found the easiest way was to take the basic incidents and to improvise them – I played all the characters in my mind and wrote down what I said to myself! In doing this I was careful to structure the dialogue and not just allow the characters to waffle. I built each scene to a small climax, remembering that anything which happened after a climax would be anti-climax and would disappoint the audience if it lasted too long. I needed, therefore, to step up the action gradually, and to take my audience with me emotionally – it is possible to lose the audience by taking too big a step; I took care to step up slowly so that they would become involved and through this emotional involvement get enjoyment. Perhaps I could leave them with something to think about afterwards, too.

One big danger I had to avoid was overwriting – trying to cram too many words into the mouths of the characters. I had to remember to give the director and actors a chance to act some meaning into the scene. For me, the best moment in *Black Roses* is scene 12 – the very short scene when Mrs Lockwood gives Tracey the flared trousers – look at the dialogue, it is minimal but if handled properly the effect on an audience can be electric.

If you ever decide to write a play, you will find, as I did, that the order in which the scenes come is important. It is desirable to vary the emotional content, too. Try to avoid having two or three angry or sad scenes all following on from one another. Take a leaf from Shakespeare's book, follow a sad scene with a lighter scene. After a sad scene the audience need to release their emotions – they may feel like crying but make them laugh and they will gladly take the opportunity to release their emotions. I was amazed how much an audience laughed at the Christmas party until I realised that it followed two quite sad scenes.

Playwriting is an enjoyable and rewarding pastime. If you follow some of these basic rules you should be able to produce some effective pieces – take a risk!

# FOLLOW-UP ACTIVITIES

## Discussion and writing

The play *Black Roses* raises many issues for you to discuss, think about and write about. It uses the true story of a group of women and their involvement in the miners' strike of 1984. This in itself is quite unusual, since history for the most part records the deeds of famous men, rarely mentioning the actions of women. The problem is obviously not that women do not do things, but that society does not value what they do.

*Black Roses* is a play which examines the relationship between the powerful and the powerless, or less powerful, most notably in the conflict between the Government and the Union. It deals with the differences between men in their workplace, and women at home. There is the theme of deprivation, and what it means to a family to lose its income and survive on charity. Yet another concern is the way in which a single event can radically change people's lives, not just at the time, but permanently. The women in this play come to see themselves in quite a different way as a result of their activities during the strike.

You might like, as a group, to talk about some of these points (and any others that occur to you) before starting the discussion and writing tasks suggested below.

- DISCUSSION
  The women end the play by singing Helen Reddy's 'I am Woman' (words pp. 22–3, 73), a song which has already been heard several times in the course of the play. Try to listen to a recording of the song.

  It is a song which has often been used by groups of women to express and strengthen pride in women's achievements. Why do you think this song has been successful in doing this? What do the words suggest to you? How important is the music in helping the impact of the song? What songs matter to you in a similar way? What is it about these songs that makes them important?

**72** *Black Roses*

- WRITING
Write your own song which celebrates something that you feel strongly about. It could be concerned with issues such as ecology or poverty, or a personal matter such as an interest, hobby or an event or feelings.

  You might like to set your song to music. There are two ways of doing this. One is to select a tune that has already been written. In *Black Roses* this happens with a chant, which is set to the tune of 'It's a long way to Tipperary'. You may find that you have to make some changes so that the words fit the phrasing of the music. Alternatively, you could write a new tune. You might like to work with a partner on this.

- DISCUSSION
In scene 7 Margaret and Maureen discuss their experiences of street-collections for money. They have encountered a number of people who are unsympathetic. What do you feel about street-collections? Are there occasions when you think it is appropriate and other occasions when you judge it to be inappropriate? Some charities and campaigns use activities such as fairs and fêtes, sponsored sports activities and raffles to raise money. What other ways are there of collecting money for a project? What are their strengths and what drawbacks do they have?

- WRITING
Often, a campaign or charity will offer people a leaflet explaining what it is that money is being raised for. You might like to collect examples of these, and read them closely to see what is said and how it is expressed.

  Choose a charity or campaign that you feel strongly about, or choose an issue which hasn't yet been used as the focus of a campaign, but which is important to you. Write your own pamphlet to be given to people to explain what it is that you are supporting. Use ideas and arguments that you think will persuade them to give money. Remember some of the things that you have learnt from the leaflets you have looked at. It isn't just a matter of copying them because you may decide that some of the wording puts people off rather than being

Black Roses 73

persuasive! You may like to include illustrations, either from your own drawings or cut from magazines. Again, look at existing examples and decide how their pictures are intended to affect the readers.

It's important always to remember that you have to have official permission to raise funds because otherwise you are begging, which is a criminal offence. You might like to find out what the procedure is to register a campaign or charity.

- DISCUSSION
  During scene 7 Maureen says 'We went into a shop this morning just to ask for a donation and that, and the bloke went mad . . . said he'd call the coppers if we didn't get out . . . They forget it's been miners what's brought 'em all their trade in the past.' Maureen is suggesting that communities have some responsibility for one another. Do you agree with this? Can you think of other examples where this applies? Does it always apply? Can the answers to society's problems always be supplied by charities, or should we take more individual responsibility?

- WRITING
  Choose an issue that you think needs attention. It may be one that you have already used in the activities above or it may be something else. Write a letter to your local paper or to your Member of Parliament, outlining the issue. After describing the problem, explain why the community or the wider population should take responsibility for this problem.

  It may be that this is a real issue that you are concerned about. In which case it might be worth making the effort to post the letter and to see what response you get.

- DISCUSSION
  During the demonstration in London, one of the women notices a sticker in a house window that proclaims 'Coal not dole'. This was a popular slogan during the miners' strike. Another was 'The miners' united will never be defeated'. What do you think is the purpose of slogans and how do you think they work? How many other slogans can you list from

**74** *Black Roses*

other campaigns and charities? Discuss how successful the slogans are, and why or how you think they function.

- WRITING
  Make a list of as many campaigns and charities that you can think of. Choose five and write your own slogans for them. Use some of the features that you have noted in other slogans, such as length and word choice – and anything else that came up in discussion. Share your slogans with the class and see how effective other people think they are.

- DISCUSSION
  Betty describes the black rose that she gives to a policeman as 'a symbol of the death of the traditional mining communities'. Why is this symbol a rose, and why is it black? What is the history of the white and red roses of Yorkshire and Lancashire? What other things can you think of that roses are used to symbolise? Why is the rose such a popular flower to use in signs and emblems? Can you think of other flowers and plants that are used for similar purposes?

- WRITING
  There does not have to be a very direct connection between a charity or campaign, and its symbol. The Labour Party, for instance, uses a red rose. The colour has a connection with the history of the labour movement, but does the rose have any significance?
  Using the list of charities and campaigns that you have already been working with, write next to them the symbols that you are aware of them using. Some may not have a symbol. Write a brief note to explain why you think the symbol was chosen or why one does not exist. Having done this, go through your list and give each campaign and charity a new symbol and offer an explanation for your choice. Try to think of a new symbol even for those campaigns which do not have one already. Why do you think they don't use one?
  Choose one of the symbols and draw your own design. Make notes that explain why the symbol has been chosen and how it might affect the public. Is the colour important? Is the

## Project

The writing of this play involved the recording of what we call 'oral history'. The playwright went and spoke and listened to the women of the Woolley mining community. He did not go to books or media reports for an official version of the events of the miners' strike. By talking with the people themselves, he was able to write from a perspective which was not often recorded in news reports. In fact, in the play and in the section called 'Writing the Play', we learn from the playwright, Steven Downs, that the mining community distrusted journalists. You might want to discuss the way in which an official account of history is shaped and why some perspectives do not get included.

In some communities people are actively collecting and publishing people's accounts of the past for oral history projects (so that their owners' contribution to the present may be understood). It is a way of making sure that voices which are not considered important enough or great enough, are heard and remembered. If there is an oral history project in your area make arrangements to talk to one of its members to find out how it operates and what it is that it aims to achieve. Perhaps it's worth going with a friend.

You possibly have friends, family or neighbours who spend a lot of time reminiscing about things that happened in their lives. Have you ever wondered whether it would be worthwhile collecting the stories and memories that you have heard from time to time and writing them down for others to read or, as in this play, to perform as a drama. You may be surprised at what you learn of the past!

- With a partner, plan your own oral history project. You will need first to decide what subject it is that you want to explore. It could be something to do with the working lives of an older generation, what people remember of their schooldays, the history of your street or neighbourhood, or a

## 76 *Black Roses*

history of an event such as a war, a disaster or a celebration.

Having decided what it is that you wish to turn into a piece of recorded history, you will need to find people who will talk with you about the events. Most people enjoy the opportunity to share their memories but some may find them painful or difficult, so be sensitive when you approach people about the project. Once they have agreed to be interviewed, agree a time and a place and warn your interviewees (the people being interviewed) that they will need to give you an hour or so without interruptions from other people or the telephone! If you are very lucky, they may be able to show you photographs and press cuttings relating to your topic. If your interviewee offers to lend you anything, remember to take very great care of the items and, if possible, copy them and return the originals straight away. If you are going to use a tape recorder, make sure it's working before you set off.

It is suggested that you do your oral history with a partner because then you can compare the impressions you have formed. This will help you shape them into the written or taped history that you are preparing.

When you have gathered all your research materials, you will need to decide the best form to present it in. You may be working towards a piece of drama or a written account or you may choose another medium, such as an (edited) audio tape, a video tape, a picture board or a journal. Whatever you choose, it may help to read Steven Downs' section on 'Writing the play', where he outlines some possibilities for giving your work a 'skeleton' or a narrative shape.

The people you interview will appreciate the opportunity of reading or seeing the finished project. Perhaps it would be most appropriate to arrange an evening in which to show the work.

### Drama ideas

Practical drama is a very good way of making connections between your own experiences and things which are completely unfamiliar and, therefore, difficult to understand. The following suggestions are intended to help you to use drama to make this link between the known and the unknown. Remember, however, that they are only suggestions – your own ideas may well be better.

- In scene 6 Tracey and her mother, Doreen, discuss the problems that Tracey has encountered at school thanks to her family's lack of money since the strike began. Tracey struggles to understand and accept that she will not be able to go on a school trip to the theatre because of the expense.

  With a partner, work on an improvisation suggested by an occasion when you have been disappointed and been unable to do something. What were the reasons for which you were unable to do the activity? Do you think they were good reasons for stopping the activity? What did it feel like at the time? How do you feel about it now? Could you have persuaded the person responsible for making the decision to change his or her mind?

- On page 19 Betty tells Jack that by the time the strike is over the men will 'be looking at us through different eyes'. By the end of the play we learn that this statement is as true for the women as it is for their miner husbands. The women understand their place in the community and in their families differently. Have there been occasions in your life where you have achieved something you never thought you would be able to do? Has this altered the way that you understand yourself?

  Share your recollections with a small group, and choose one with good dramatic possibilities. Improvise scenes around 'the before', 'the during' and 'the after' of the event. The roles played by the other group members should show different attitudes towards the central character. Some may be supportive, others critical. Can you show why people react as they do? Do people's judgements change after the event?

  When you are happy with your improvisations for each character choose the single line which you think best represents their position. You might like to speak these lines to an audience and see if they can work out the situation, the characters and the event.

- After the confrontation with the police, Sandra observes that the miners have 'played right into their hands today'. Ray is unwilling to take any responsibility for the violent clash and says that it was due to 'agitators and students' who 'started the trouble'. This leads to the women planning their own demonstration, which Christine hopes will 'show the human side of the struggle . . . how families is struggling together . . .'. Sandra says it will be 'nowt violent' but a 'peaceful protest'.

  As a large group, think of incidents in your own lives where the intention was to put your case but somehow it ended in a confrontation rather than a discussion. It could, for example, involve trying to explain a classroom accident to a teacher, or a disagreement between groups over sharing space in a youth club or on school grounds. When you have re-enacted the original incident, work on reshaping it so that it has a positive outcome. How can you make your new ending believable?

### Designing the play

Putting on a production of *Black Roses* requires some work in collecting costumes and props. This, of course, needs thought and planning. The action of the play moves from space to space, so you may choose to show the setting by using props rather than realistic scenery. It is probably worth going to the library to research some details about mining communities and mining lives before you begin to design or gather props.

- Design the clothing the miners are likely to be wearing on picket duty. Remember, this is rather different from the clothing they might wear at work. Use the hints the play gives you. Think about the characters' lifestyles, the place in which they live, the seasons and the family incomes. Try sketching an outfit for Jack.

  Are your costumes to be highly realistic or do they use simple props like hats and scarves to hint at the dress of a person? If you are only going to hint at the costume of a character, what will the base outfit for the actor be? Where

will you get this clothing from? Will you make any of it?
What sort of cost is involved? Is there a budget to pay for
these costumes and does it limit what you can do?

- Pickets and demonstrators often carry placards or banners.
  Some are simple makeshift affairs that carry a message such as
  'Coal not dole'. Others involve a lot of skill and work, such
  as official union banners, which often carry a coat of arms or
  logo worked in embroidery or appliqué. Design some of the
  placards and banners you might use. You might do some
  research to find the coats of arms or logos that were actually
  used. The Nottingham branch of the National Union of
  Miners used an image of a pick-axe with two fists clenched
  around its handle. Can you discover what image the
  Yorkshire miners used?
  Choose one of your designs and make your own placard.
  You will need to choose your materials, and one of your
  considerations will be cost. For this reason you may want to
  use scrap materials. Discarded estate agents' boards are often
  used to make placards. The material they are made from is
  much more durable than corrugated cardboard.

### Rehearsing the play

Every production involves a great deal of rehearsal. At the
beginning this may take the form of reading through and
discussing characters and situations so that each member of the
cast can offer ideas and learn from others. Then there will come
a period in which the play is 'blocked'; this is where each actor
is told by the director where to enter and exit from the stage and
what movements need to be made during each scene. From then
on it is a matter of everyone collaborating to build the
characterisation and the flow of the play so that it holds
together as a dramatic piece.

- Make your own notes about the character you are to play.
  Look closely at the script for the sort of person that you
  think you are and what this may mean for how you act your
  part. For instance, in the early scenes, Jack is not very

impressed by the idea that the women will do anything other than the cooking and housekeeping for the miners. What sort of attitudes do you think he holds towards women in general?

- Choose a particular scene and work out your own blocking. It is important that you have a sense of the space that the performance will happen in and where the furniture and props will be so that you have the actors moving both for their character's actions and within the possible space. You might like to draw a ground-plan (a bird's-eye view) of the stage before you start. You could either mark your copy of the script with the notes about blocking, or photocopy the scene and write on the copy. Use the language of stage directions such as 'upstage' and 'downstage'. (Incidentally, make sure you know which is stage left and which is stage right!) If you are performing 'in the round' (where the audience is on all sides) it is more difficult to label the acting area so you will probably have to use letters or numbers to label the entrances.